THE BOOK OF

SPANISH
COOKING

THE BOOK OF

SPANISH
COOKING

HILAIRE WALDEN

Photographed by
JON STEWART

HPBooks
a division of
PRICE STERN SLOAN
Los Angeles

ANOTHER BEST SELLING VOLUME FROM HPBOOKS

HPBooks
A division of Price Stern Sloan, Inc.
11150 Olympic Boulevard
Suite 650
Los Angeles, California 90064

9 8 7 6 5 4 3 2 1

ISBN 1-55788-063-8

By arrangement with Salamander Books Ltd.

© Salamander Books Ltd., 1993

Home Economists: Kerenza Harries and Jo Craig
Printed in Belgium by Proost International Book Production

CONTENTS

INTRODUCTION 7

SPANISH COOKING 8

TAPAS 12

SOUPS 40

EGG DISHES 44

FISH DISHES 48

POULTRY & GAME DISHES 65

MEAT DISHES 79

RICE & LEGUME DISHES 92

VEGETABLE DISHES 99

SWEET DISHES 108

SAUCES, ACCOMPANIMENTS & DRINKS 114

INDEX 120

INTRODUCTION

The Spanish cuisine is one of the most exciting, rewarding and varied in the world as it encompasses dishes that contain a kaleidoscope of ingredients, prepared in myriad styles to perfectly suit every occasion, taste and diet. *The Book of Spanish Cooking* brings you the best examples of all these styles.

There are simple dishes flavored with herbs, vibrantly colored and richly flavored meat and poultry dishes and equally delicious vegetable versions, as well as some dishes that are light and quick-cooking. There are also dishes based on rice and legumes that are ideal one-dish meals, plus warming, hearty soups contrasted by those that are the epitome of summer eating.

There are fish recipes to serve for sophisticated eating or family suppers, with eggs for snacks and plenty of cakes and pastries to satisfy those with a sweet tooth.

The Spanish cuisine is essentially a family one, developed out of the ingenious exploitation of accessible local raw materials, and the imaginative and best use of foods that were readily available.

Based on simple ingredients, with its roots firmly in home cooking and pure country food, Spanish cooking is essentially hearty and unpretentious; ingredients are inexpensive, flavors direct, recipes easy and presentation straightforward with no unnecessary show. The criteria for the success of a dish is whether it tastes good.

In line with the trend that exists in respect to other national cuisines, such as French and Italian, both Spaniards and foreigners are now taking a closer look at "traditional" Spanish food, increasing its reputation and expanding awareness of it. There is a growing band of "new wave" chefs who are researching old dishes, refining them to suit modern tastes, and making Spanish food fashionable.

True, traditional Spanish cooking is many faceted. Indigenous foods and traditional culinary practices have been reinforced throughout the country's long history by the absorption of new ingredients and cultural influences from many different countries. The Romans left their imprint, principally in the irrigation of parts of the east coast, and the introduction of olives, while 700 years of Moorish occupation resulted in almonds, citrus fruits and fragrant spices becoming integral ingredients in Spanish cooking. The discovery of the New World resulted in the introduction, and wide acceptance, of tomatoes, sweet and hot peppers, zucchini, many types of beans, potatoes, chocolate and vanilla.

Furthermore, Spain covers areas as diverse as sparse mountain ranges, arid plains, fertile orchards and arable lands, olive and fruit groves, regions that are cold and wet, and those that are hot and dry, coasts facing two different seas—the Mediterranean and the Atlantic—and many rivers. Not surprisingly, each different area yields different foods and calls for a different type of cooking.

However, there are a number of ingredients and flavors that distinguish Spanish food. The olive is vital, particularly for its oil; Spain is the greatest consumer of olive oil in the world. Garlic is an indispensable element in the majority of dishes. Parsley is a popular herb, and nuts appear frequently, often ground to make a sauce. Onions, green and red peppers and tomatoes are the other constants.

FOOD OF THE REGIONS
The Basque province has both wonderful fish and seafood from the Atlantic Ocean and some of the finest cattle, sheep and dairy foods in Spain. Portions are large, as is to be expected in a cold climate, but the cooking has a certain refinement. Dishes cooked al chilindron, in a flavorful sauce based on the particularly good local red bell peppers, and tomatoes, onions and garlic, are typical of Navarra and Aragon. Trout from the clear mountain streams that rise in the Pyrenees are a regional favorite, especially cooked with ham.

The food of Catalonia is exciting and richly varied and features interesting sauces, such as Romesco (see page 114) and Garlic Sauce (see page 34), aromatic herbs and noticeable similarities with French Mediterranean food, such as Zarzuela (see page 62), a close cousin of bouillabaise.

Valencia and Murcia form one of the most densely populated and richest agricultural areas of Europe, and exhibit distinct Moorish influences. Here there are groves of oranges and almonds, large market gardens and rice fields. The last two provide the ingredients for authentic Paella Valenciana—the addition of fish and shellfish is a modern adaptation that has become universally popular. Andulusia is the land of olives, olive oil and sizzling fried foods, particularly the varied sea and shellfish from around the long coastline. In contrast, Extremadura is a land of tough, hardy countrymen, and simple hearty cooking with many stew-type dishes. The vast, exposed Central Plain produces Spain's most well-known cheese, Manchego (see page 9) as well as many other sheep milk cheeses. The area is most generally thought of as a land of roasts.

Galicia and Asturias are renowned for the quality of the fish and shellfish, and as the home of excellent Empanadas (see page 24). The climate is comparatively cold and wet, so appetites tend to be hearty and dishes correspondingly filling.

EATING PATTERNS
The traditional breakfast is usually eaten in cafes and consists of churros with large cups of hot chocolate in which the churros are dunked. Coffee and sweet cakes or a light snack are eaten at mid-morning. Lunch, the main meal of the day, is at 2 o'clock, but is often preceded by tapas, usually taken at a bar or cafe on the way to home or to a restaurant. Work begins again in the late afternoon. About 6 o'clock is the time for a merienda, a light snack. Tapas are usually eaten from 8 until 10 o'clock, when it is time for dinner. This is usually lighter than lunch.

TAPAS
Originally, and still in some bars today, tapas were simply a few olives or almonds, and perhaps a selection of cheeses, sausages and serrano ham and possibly cubes of tortilla served, often free, to accompany a glass of fino

sherry. But nowadays, tapas have come to encompass more or less any hot or cold dish that can be served in small portions, and they may be quite substantial. They are displayed along the length of the counter of a bar or cafe to be ordered in a group.

Although quintessentially Spanish, tapas are so well-suited to today's style of casual eating that they have caught the popular imagination outside Spain. A selection of tapas is ideal for an interesting informal meal, and they are wonderful fare for a party, buffet, picnic or barbecue.

INGREDIENTS

Cheese: Although Spain produces about 200 cheeses, only Manchego enjoys any degree of renown, and is the only one exported in quantity. Manchego may be mild and quite soft, or strong and hard. It is made from sheep milk, so is quite expensive. If Manchego is not available, use freshly cut Parmesan cheese as an acceptable alternative.

Chiles: These play an important role in Spanish cooking, adding not only heat but distinct flavor to dishes. Different varieties of chiles impart different flavors and degree of heat. Generally, large chiles are milder than small ones, while dried ones are often hotter than fresh. Red chiles are ripened green chiles, and so they have a sweeter, more rounded flavor compared to the fresher, "green" taste of the immature form. Chile seeds are not only hotter than the flesh, but have less flavor so are generally removed.

A little care is needed when handling chiles; avoid touching your eyes and any cuts or sensitive areas, and always wash hands thoroughly afterward. If you have sensitive skin, it is advisable to wear rubber gloves.

Chorizo: The best chorizo contains as much as 95 percent pork. Other ingredients are pork fat, salt, garlic and paprika, which gives it the pronounced red color. The most widely known and available chorizos are fully cured and can be eaten without cooking, for example, sliced onto bread, as a tapas or in salads. The two degrees of spiciness are *picante* (hot) and *dulce* (mild).

The other type of chorizo, which has to be cooked, is found in stews and in bean and potato dishes, which will be colored red by the leeching out of the paprika in the chorizo. These chorizos are short and stubby and come linked together in the same way as sausages. They sometimes have added flavor from being smoked over oak fires. Oregano is also sometimes added.

For the best and truest flavor, use good Spanish chorizo, but if they are not available use Italian sausages, usually found in Italian delicatessens.

Garlic: This is essential in Spanish cooking. Use the freshest possible—if there is any sign of a green shoot in the center of a clove, remove it as it imparts a bitter taste to a dish. Buy garlic bulbs that are plump and firm and store them in a cool, dry place. Raw garlic has a pungent flavor, but when it is cooked, the taste mellows to give a subtle background flavor, and whole cloves can be eaten. Chopping garlic gives a more pronounced flavor than crushing it.

Herbs: Parsley is an important herb in Spanish cooking. The flat-leaved type is used. Oregano makes an occasional appearance, while bay leaves and thyme are quite widely used, especially in dishes which require long cooking. The presence of mint, most popularly with fava beans and chicken, is a legacy left by the Moors. Fresh herbs give a better flavor then dried ones. If you do have to use dried herbs, however, reduce the amount in the recipes by one-half to two-thirds.

Ham: The most well-known Spanish ham is *jamon serrano*. This is a raw, air-dried ham and is often eaten in thin, though not wafer thin, slices carved along the grain as a tapa. The best *jamon serrano* comes from the black Iberian pig, but the supply is limited. *Jamon serrano* is also used for cooking, when it is more thickly sliced so it can be chopped into chunks. Italian prosciutto is the nearest substitute.

Olive oil: Olive oil lends a characteristic flavor to many dishes. For general cooking, use a pure Spanish olive oil as it has a mild flavor, and keep the more

distinctly flavored, and more expensive, virgin oils for dressings. Keep olive oil in a cool, dark place, but not the refrigerator, and use within a year.

Onions: Yellow Spanish onions have a sweet and mild taste.

Paprika: *Pimenton dulce*, produced from ground dried red bell peppers, is an essential element in Spanish cooking, adding a characteristic flavor and color to many dishes. It is added at the beginning of the cooking and is fried to release its flavor. However, it should not be overheated or it will taste burnt.

Peppers: These come in progressive stages of ripening, from green through to red, but red ones, being the ripest, are sweeter and more rounded in flavor.

To remove the skin from peppers, either broil halved peppers skin side up, 2 inches away from the broiler 8 to 10 minutes, or bake them in an oven preheated to 400F (205C) 20 to 40 minutes, until they are blistered and charred (this also adds a delicious smoky flavor), then leave until cool enough to handle and scrape or peel off the skin.

Thin-skinned, small, long and pointed *piquillo* peppers are the ones that are used for stuffing; they are sold in bottles, which are generally best, or in cans. If unavailable, substitute ordinary canned small red peppers.

Dark-red *nora* peppers are sold dried and can be seen in Spain in strings hanging from windows or in markets or grocers. They do not have much flesh, but their flavor and color is concentrated. To use them, pull out the stem and shake out as many seeds as possible. Soak them in cold water 30 to 60 minutes to soften the skin, then cut in half and scrape out the flesh using a teaspoon. Paprika pepper can be substituted for *noras*.

Rice: Spanish rice is medium-grain, similar to Italian arborio rice, but whereas a risotto is stirred to encourage the rice grains to becomes sticky, the rice for a paella must be left undisturbed during cooking.

Saffron: Although expensive, only a few threads are needed to give a wonderful flavor and aroma to a dish for four people. For the best flavor, use genuine Spanish saffron threads or

strands, and avoid saffron powder as it may have added ingredients that give color but no flavor. To gain maximum flavor from saffron, crush the threads with a small pestle and mortar or between two teaspoons, then soak in a little hot water.

Sherry vinegar: This is made from Spanish sherry, and is rich and concentrated, so very little is needed to enhance the flavor of a dish.

Tomatoes: Well-flavored tomatoes are important to the success of many Spanish dishes. For the recipes in this book use beefsteak tomatoes. To skin tomatoes, put them in a bowl, cover with boiling water, leave about 30 seconds, place in cold water, then remove from the water one at a time and slip off the skin.

EQUIPMENT
Spanish cooks use few pieces of equipment but three feature prominently.

Mortar and pestle: This is used extensively, but the end of a rolling pin and a small bowl can be substituted for crushing spices and small amounts of ingredients, and a small blender or food processor can cope with larger volumes.

Cazuelas: Cazuelas are flameproof earthenware casseroles that are unglazed outside and glazed inside. They are the most commonly used pieces of cooking equipment in Spain, being used for all manner of cooking processes as they cook evenly, hold the heat well and are inert, so do not taint food. Cazuelas are available in a wide variety of shapes, sizes and depths from fairly shallow small ones for individual portions of tapas, to deep ones used for poultry and meat casseroles. It is wise to use a heat diffuser when cooking on top of the stove as direct contact with heat can cause a cazuela to crack.

A cazuela should be seasoned before using it for the first time to avoid cracking: half fill with water and a generous splash of vinegar, bring gently to a boil, then boil until the liquid has evaporated. Cazuelas rarely have lids but foil can be used for a covering, if necessary.

Paella: Although a wide skillet can be used for making paellas, a proper paella pan with a thick metal base and sloping sides will assist in making really successful ones. Moreover, if cooking for 4 or more, it is unlikely that you will have a sufficiently large skillet—a 16-inch one is necessary for 4 servings, a 20-inch one for 6 to 8.

STUFFED MUSSELS

3 pounds large mussels in their shells
1/3 cup dry white wine
1/3 cup olive oil
1/2 cup fresh bread crumbs
3 tablespoon finely chopped fresh parsley
1 tablespoon finely chopped fresh oregano
2 garlic cloves, finely crushed
Pinch of red (cayenne) pepper
Salt and freshly ground black pepper
1 large lemon, quartered
Parsley sprigs, to garnish

Scrub mussels and remove beards. Discard any mussels that remain open when tapped firmly. Into a large saucepan, put mussels and wine.

Cover and boil 4 to 5 minutes, shaking pan occasionally, until shells open. Strain and reserve liquid. Discard any shells that do not open. Discard top shells, leaving mussels on remaining shells. In a small bowl, stir together 3 tablespoons oil, the bread crumbs, herbs, garlic, cayenne, salt and pepper. If mixture is dry, moisten with a little of the reserved mussel cooking liquid.

Preheat broiler. Divide bread-crumb mixture among mussels on their shells. Place on a baking sheet. Drizzle with remaining olive oil and broil 1 to 2 minutes or until topping is crisp and golden. Squeeze lemon juice over mussels and serve garnished with parsley sprigs.

Makes 4 to 6 servings.

SIZZLING SHRIMP

1/2 cup olive oil
4 garlic cloves, finely crushed
1 small fresh red chile, seeded and chopped
3/4 pound raw shrimp, shelled
Sea salt
2 tablespoons chopped fresh parsley
Lemon wedges and bread, to serve

In 4 individual flameproof dishes over high heat, heat oil. Add garlic and chile and cook 1 to 2 minutes, then add shrimp and sea salt.

Cook 2 to 3 minutes, stirring occasionally. Stir in parsley. Serve quickly so the shrimp are sizzling in the oil, and accompany with lemon wedges and bread to mop up the juices.

Makes 4 servings.

Note: One large dish, or a skillet, can be used instead of individual dishes.

BROILED SHRIMP

1 pound raw jumbo shrimp, shelled with tails left on
5 tablespoons extra-virgin olive oil
1/2 garlic clove, finely crushed
Juice of 1 lemon
Salt and pepper
1 small beefsteak tomato, peeled, seeded and finely
   chopped
1/2 small, fresh red chile, finely chopped
1 tablespoon finely chopped fresh parsley
Parsley sprigs and lemon slices and zest, to garnish

Using a small sharp knife, make a cut along back of each shrimp and remove black vein. Thread shrimp onto 4 skewers and place in a shallow dish. In a small bowl, stir together 2 tablespoons of the oil, the garlic, 1-1/2 tablespoons lemon juice, salt and pepper. Pour over shrimp and let stand 30 minutes.

Preheat broiler. Lift shrimp from dish and place on broiler rack. Brush with any liquid remaining in dish and broil 3 to 4 minutes until bright pink. In another small bowl, stir together remaining oil and lemon juice, tomato, chile, parsley, salt and pepper. Spoon over hot shrimp and serve garnished with parsley and lemon slices and zest.

Makes 4 servings.

Note: If using bamboo or wooden skewers, soak in water 30 minutes before using.

SHRIMP IN OVERCOATS

1 pound jumbo shrimp, shelled with tails left on.
1/2 lemon
Salt and pepper
1-3/4 cups all-purpose flour
2 cups light ale or beer
Olive oil for deep-frying
Lemon and lime wedges and fresh dill, to garnish

Using a small sharp knife, make a cut along back of each shrimp and remove the black vein. Squeeze lemon juice over shrimp and season lightly. Set aside 15 minutes.

In a bowl, stir together flour and a small pinch of salt. Slowly whisk in ale or beer to make a smooth, thick batter.

Two-thirds fill a deep-fryer with oil and heat to 350F (175C). Pat shrimp dry with paper towels. Pick up each shrimp in turn by its tail and dip in batter; do not cover tail. Lower into oil and fry about 4 minutes or until crisp and golden. Drain on paper towels and serve hot.

Makes 4 servings.

TUNA CROQUETTES

1 (15-1/2 oz.) can tuna in water
About 1 cup milk
2 tablespoons olive oil, plus extra for deep-frying
1/4 Spanish onion, finely chopped
4 tablespoons all-purpose flour
1-1/2 tablespoons finely chopped fresh parsley
2 tablespoons lemon juice
3 eggs, beaten
Salt and pepper
3 cups fresh bread crumbs
Lemon wedges and watercress, to serve

Drain tuna and add enough milk to liquid to make 1-1/2 cups. Flake tuna; set aside.

In a small saucepan, heat 1 tablespoon of the olive oil. Add onion and cook about 4 minutes or until soft but not colored. Stir in flour and cook, stirring, 2 minutes. Remove from heat and slowly stir in half the milk mixture. Return to heat and bring to a boil, stirring in remaining milk mixture. Simmer 8 minutes, stirring occasionally. Remove from heat; stir in tuna, parsley, lemon juice, 1 egg, salt and pepper.

Into a shallow dish, pour tuna mixture. Cool, cover and refrigerate 2 to 3 hours. Put remaining eggs and the bread crumbs into separate bowls. Lightly beat eggs. Dip small balls of tuna mixture first in egg, then bread crumbs to coat evenly. Half fill a deep-fryer with oil and heat to 350F (175C). Fry tuna balls in batches 2 to 3 minutes until crisp and golden. Using a slotted spoon, transfer to paper towels to drain. Serve hot with lemon wedges and watercress.

Makes 4 servings.

STUFFED SQUID

1-1/2 to 2 pounds small squid
4 anchovy fillets, canned in oil, drained
2 ounces blanched almonds, toasted and chopped, or 6
   ripe olives, pitted and chopped
1 garlic clove, crushed
1-1/2 tablespoons mixed chopped fresh parsley and
   oregano
1 egg, beaten
1 tablespoon ground blanched almonds
Salt and paprika
3 tablespoons olive oil
Juice of 1/2 lemon
Lemon slices, sliced pitted ripe olives and fresh herb
   sprigs, to garnish

Preheat oven to 350F (175C). To prepare squid, with a sharp knife, cut off fins. Pull bag and tentacles apart. Remove sword-shaped pen and viscera from bag. Cut head away from tentacles and discard. Rinse bag and tentacles thoroughly under cold running water. Chop tentacles finely and place in a small bowl. Using a fork, mix in anchovies, then chopped almonds or olives, garlic, herbs, egg and ground almonds. Season with salt and paprika.

Fill squid with anchovy mixture, secure openings with wooden picks, then place in a single layer in a shallow baking dish. Sprinkle with salt and paprika, then pour the oil and lemon juice over the squid. Bake about 30 minutes or until tender. Serve garnished with lemon slices, ripe olives and herbs.

Makes 4 to 6 servings.

GREEN MUSSEL SALAD

3 pounds mussels in their shells
1/2 cup extra-virgin olive oil
2 tablespoons white-wine vinegar
2 teaspoons capers, well drained
2 tablespoons finely chopped Spanish onion
1/2 garlic clove, finely chopped
2 tablespoons chopped fresh parsley
1 teaspoon paprika
Small pinch of red (cayenne) pepper
Salt

Clean mussels (see page 12) and discard any that are open. Into a large saucepan, put mussels with 5 tablespoons water. Cover pan and boil 4 to 5 minutes, shaking pan occasionally or until shells open. Drain mussels and discard any that remain closed. Remove mussels from shells and discard shells.

In a bowl, mix together remaining ingredients. Stir in mussels, cover and refrigerate overnight. Return to room temperature before serving.

Makes 4 servings.

TUNA SALAD

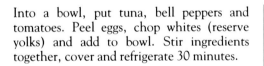

1 (7-oz.) can tuna in water, drained and flaked
1 large green bell pepper, diced
1 large red bell pepper, diced
3 beefsteak tomatoes, peeled, seeded and diced
2 large hard-cooked eggs
1 thin slice day-old bread, crusts removed
1 garlic clove, finely chopped
Salt and black pepper
1-1/2 tablespoons red-wine vinegar
3 tablespoons olive oil
Crisp lettuce leaves, to serve
Fresh parsley, to garnish

Into a bowl, put tuna, bell peppers and tomatoes. Peel eggs, chop whites (reserve yolks) and add to bowl. Stir ingredients together, cover and refrigerate 30 minutes.

Soak bread in cold water, then squeeze out. Using a small blender or mortar and pestle, mix garlic to a paste with salt and hard-cooked egg yolks. Mix in bread, vinegar and black pepper. Slowly mix in oil to make a smooth cream. Pour over salad and refrigerate 30 minutes. To serve, toss salad gently and arrange on crisp lettuce leaves. Garnish with parsley.

Makes 6 servings.

─── MARINATED SARDINES ───

1 pound fresh sardines or anchovies, cleaned
Sea salt and freshly ground black pepper
1/2 cup white-wine vinegar
1 garlic clove, finely crushed
2 tablespoons finely chopped Spanish onion
3 tablespoons olive oil
2 teaspoons fresh lemon juice
Diced red bell pepper and chopped fresh parsley, to
  garnish

Place 1 fish skin-side up on work surface and press thumbs firmly along backbone; turn fish over, pull out backbone from head and cut free at tail. Repeat with remaining fish.

In a shallow, nonmetallic dish, lay fish in a single layer. Sprinkle sea salt, vinegar, garlic and onion over fish. Cover and refrigerate overnight. Drain and rinse fish, reserving some of onion. Pat fish dry on paper towels, then place on a serving plate. In a small bowl, mix together oil, lemon juice, reserved onion and salt and pepper. Pour over fish and garnish with diced red pepper and parsley.

Makes 4 servings.

CHEESE FRITTERS

Olive oil for deep-frying
2 egg whites
1 cup finely grated mature Manchego or Parmesan
  cheese
1 cup fresh bread crumbs
About 1 tablespoon finely chopped fresh herbs, such as
  parsley, chives and thyme
Salt, pepper and paprika
Thyme sprigs, to garnish

In a deep-fryer two-thirds filled with olive oil, heat oil to 350F (175C).

Meanwhile, in a bowl, whisk egg whites until stiff but not dry. Lightly fold in cheese, bread crumbs and herbs. Season with salt, pepper and paprika.

Form egg white mixture into small walnut-size balls, adding balls to hot oil as they are shaped. Fry each about 3 minutes or until golden. Transfer to paper towels to drain. Serve hot, garnished with thyme.

Makes 4 servings.

—BELL PEPPER & ONION TART—

2 cups bread flour
Salt and pepper
1 teaspoon active dry yeast
2/3 cup warm milk
1 egg yolk
4 tablespoons olive oil
1 pound Spanish onions, halved and sliced
4 red bell peppers, sliced
4 yellow bell peppers, sliced
About 1/2 cup fresh thyme, oregano and parsley sprigs
16 to 20 canned anchovy fillets, drained

Into a bowl, sift flour and salt. Stir in yeast.

Stir milk into egg yolk, then slowly pour into flour, stirring constantly. Beat 5 to 10 minutes or until dough comes cleanly away from bowl.

Turn dough onto a lightly floured surface and knead until smooth and elastic. Form into a ball, place in an oiled bowl, cover and leave in a warm place about 1 hour until doubled in size.

Meanwhile, in a skillet, heat 3 tablespoons of the oil, add onions, peppers and herbs and cook over medium heat, stirring occasionally, 20 to 25 minutes or until vegetables are soft but not browned. Add a few tablespoons water if necessary to prevent browning. Season with salt and pepper and set aside.

Preheat oven to 475F (240C). On a lightly floured surface, punch down and flatten dough. Roll out to a 12-inch circle. Carefully transfer to an oiled baking sheet. Turn up edge to make a rim. Prick well with a fork.

Spread vegetable mixture over dough, arrange anchovy fillets on top, drizzle with remaining oil and bake 25 to 30 minutes or until the dough is well risen, crisp and golden. Serve warm.

Makes 6 servings.

EMPANADA

4 cups bread flour
Salt
2 teaspoons active dry yeast
1-1/4 cups warm milk
2 egg yolks
Dash of anise extract
1 egg, beaten
FILLING:
2 tablespoons olive oil
2 Spanish onions, chopped
8 ounces beefsteak tomatoes
1 (14-oz.) can tuna in oil, drained
1 large red bell pepper
6 ripe olives, pitted and quartered
4 saffron threads

Into a bowl, sift flour and a pinch of salt. Stir in yeast. Stir milk into egg yolks, add anise, then slowly pour into flour, stirring constantly. Beat 5 to 10 minutes or until dough comes cleanly away from bowl.

Turn dough out on a lightly floured surface and knead until smooth and elastic. Form into 2 equal-size balls, place in an oiled bowl, cover and leave in a warm place about 1 hour or until doubled in size.

To make filling, in a skillet, heat oil. Add onions and cook, stirring occasionally, about 4 minutes or until softened. Peel, seed and chop tomatoes, stir into pan and simmer until thickened. Flake tuna. Chop bell pepper and stir into pan with tuna and olives. Crush saffron threads and dissolve in 2 tablespoons hot water. Add to pan. Simmer until bubbly, then set aside.

Preheat oven to 400F (205C). Grease a baking sheet. On a lightly floured surface, roll out each piece of dough to a thin rectangle or square. Transfer 1 piece to baking sheet.

Spread filling over dough, leaving a narrow border all the way around. Dampen border with water. Cover with remaining piece of dough and press edges together. Glaze with beaten egg and cut a slit in center. Bake 15 to 20 minutes or until golden. Serve warm, cut into rectangles or squares.

Makes 4 to 6 servings.

KIDNEYS IN SHERRY

1 pound lamb kidneys
3 tablespoons olive oil
2 garlic cloves, chopped
2 cups chopped mushrooms
2 ounces serrano ham, sliced
Salt and pepper
6 to 8 tablespoons fino sherry
Fresh parsley, to garnish

With a sharp knife, remove skin from outside of kidneys. Cut each kidney in half lengthwise, then snip out and discard cores. Quarter kidneys, then set aside.

In a skillet, heat oil. Add garlic and cook 2 to 3 minutes. Stir in mushrooms and ham and fry until liquid from mushrooms has evaporated.

Stir kidneys into pan and fry 2 to 3 minutes, stirring frequently, so kidneys are lightly browned on outside and still pink in center. Add seasoning and sherry and boil, stirring occasionally, until sherry has almost evaporated. Garnish with parsley and serve hot.

Makes 4 servings.

SPICY PORK KABOBS

2 teaspoons paprika
1 teaspoon finely crushed coriander seeds
1-1/2 teaspoons ground cumin
1 teaspoon finely chopped fresh oregano
1/4 teaspoon ground ginger
Large pinch each ground cinnamon, red (cayenne)
    pepper and grated nutmeg
1 bay leaf, finely crumbled
2 tablespoons olive oil
Salt and pepper
1 pound boned loin of pork
Lemon slices and fresh bay leaves, to garnish

In a bowl, mix together all ingredients, except pork and garnish. Cut pork into 1-inch cubes, add to marinade and stir to coat evenly. Cover bowl and refrigerate 8 to 12 hours, turning pork occasionally.

Preheat broiler. Thread pork onto small skewers. Cook under hot broiler about 7 minutes, turning occasionally, or until pork is cooked through but still juicy. Garnish with lemon slices and bay leaves and serve hot.

Makes 4 servings.

SPICED OLIVES

1 pound green or ripe olives
1 fresh oregano sprig
1 fresh thyme sprig
1 teaspoon finely chopped fresh rosemary
2 bay leaves
1 teaspoon fennel seeds, bruised
1 teaspoon finely crushed cumin seeds
1 fresh red chile, seeded and chopped
4 garlic cloves, crushed
Olive oil

Using a small sharp knife, make a lengthwise slit through to pit of each olive. Put olives into a bowl. Stir in oregano, thyme, rosemary, bay leaves, fennel seeds, cumin seeds, chile and garlic.

Into a jar with a tight-fitting lid, pack olive mixture. Add enough oil to cover olives, seal and leave at least 3 days, shaking jar occasionally, before using.

Makes 6 servings.

—MUSHROOMS WITH GARLIC—

3 tablespoons olive oil
2 garlic cloves, finely chopped
8 cups (1 pound) coarsely chopped mushrooms
1/4 cup fino sherry
1/2 cup pine nuts
Squeeze of lemon juice
Salt and pepper
2 tablespoons chopped fresh parsley

In a large skillet, heat oil. Add garlic and cook over medium-high heat about 3 minutes or until just beginning to brown.

Stir mushrooms, sherry and pine nuts into pan and continue cooking until mushroom juices have almost evaporated. Add lemon juice and seasonings to taste, then stir in parsley and serve.

Makes 4 servings.

MUSHROOMS WITH ANCHOVIES

1/2 cup crumbled fresh bread without crusts
1/4 cup milk
1 pound medium-size flat button mushrooms
4 bacon slices, finely chopped
4 canned anchovy fillets, finely chopped
1 garlic clove, finely chopped
1 egg, beaten
3 tablespoons finely chopped fresh parsley
Pinch of chopped fresh oregano
Salt and pepper
1/4 cup dry bread crumbs
1/4 cup olive oil
Fresh oregano, to garnish

Preheat oven to 400F (205C). Oil a large baking sheet. Into a small bowl put bread. Add milk and let soak. Remove stems from mushrooms and chop finely. Put into a bowl with bacon, anchovy fillets, garlic, egg, parsley, oregano, salt and pepper. Squeeze soaked bread dry, add to bacon mixture and mix together well.

Divide bread mixture among mushrooms, piling mixture into small mounds. Place on baking sheet and sprinkle with bread crumbs. Drizzle oil over mushrooms. Bake on top shelf of oven 20 to 30 minutes or until top of stuffing is crisp. Let stand a few minutes before serving; garnish with oregano.

Makes 4 to 6 servings.

──── SHRIMP-STUFFED EGGS ────

4 hard-cooked eggs, peeled
1/4 cup mayonnaise
2 ounces shelled cooked shrimps, chopped
Salt, red (cayenne) pepper and lemon juice, to taste
Lettuce leaves, to serve
Whole shrimp, paprika and fresh parsley sprigs, to
    garnish

With a sharp knife, slice eggs in half lengthwise. Using a teaspoon, scoop the yolks into a bowl, reserving the whites.

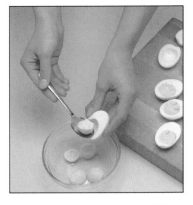

Add mayonnaise to yolks and, using a fork, mash with the yolks and shrimp. Add salt, cayenne and lemon juice.

Divide shrimp mixture among egg whites. Arrange on lettuce leaves and garnish with whole shrimp, paprika and parsley sprigs.

Makes 4 servings.

FRIED CAULIFLOWER

1 small head cauliflower (about 1-1/2 pounds)
1/3 cup all-purpose flour
1/3 cup freshly grated Manchego or Parmesan cheese
  (1-1/2 ounces)
Salt and pepper
1 egg, beaten
1/2 cup light ale or beer
Olive oil for deep-frying
Chopped fresh herbs, to garnish

In a saucepan of boiling salted water, cook cauliflower about 20 minutes or until tender but still very firm. Drain and divide into flowerets. Cut each floweret in half.

Into a small bowl, put flour, cheese, pepper and a little salt. Stir together, then form a well in center. Pour egg into well. Gradually pour in ale or beer, drawing dry ingredients into liquids. Let stand 30 minutes.

Half fill a deep-fryer or a pan with olive oil and heat to 350F (175C). Dip 2 or 3 pieces of cauliflower into batter, allowing excess batter to flow off, then slip them into pan. Add more pieces to pan, but do not crowd. Cook 2 to 3 minutes until cauliflower is golden, then using a slotted spoon, transfer to paper towels to drain. Continue until all cauliflower has been cooked. Serve hot, garnished with chopped fresh herbs.

Makes 6 to 8 servings.

—— FRIED STUFFED PEPPERS ——

9 ounces ground chicken
2 bacon slices, chopped
1-1/2 cups finely chopped button mushrooms
1 garlic clove, finely chopped
1 tablespoon olive oil, plus extra for frying
2 tablespoons all-purpose flour
3 tablespoons milk
2-1/2 tablespoons finely chopped fresh parsley
Pinch of freshly grated nutmeg
12 to 16 bottled or canned small red peppers, drained
2 large eggs, beaten
1 recipe Tomato Sauce (page 115), to serve
Fresh parsley sprigs, to garnish

In a bowl, mix together chicken, bacon, mushrooms and garlic. In a skillet, heat the 1 tablespoon oil. Add chicken mixture and cook, stirring occasionally, 2 to 3 minutes. Stir in flour, cook 2 minutes, then stir in milk, parsley and nutmeg. Cook 2 to 3 minutes, stirring frequently. Cool, then use mixture to stuff peppers.

Put eggs in a shallow bowl and seasoned flour in another shallow bowl. Dip peppers in egg, then in flour to coat lightly and evenly. In a skillet, heat 1/4 to 1/2 inch of oil. Add peppers and fry until evenly browned, about 4 minutes, turning peppers carefully. Using a slotted spoon, transfer to paper towels to drain. Serve hot with Tomato Sauce. Garnish with parsley.

Makes 4 servings.

POTATOES WITH GARLIC SAUCE

1 pound small potatoes, preferably new, unpeeled
Sea salt
1 tablespoon finely chopped fresh parsley
GARLIC SAUCE:
6 to 9 garlic cloves
Salt and pepper
About 2/3 cup olive oil

Add potatoes to a saucepan of boiling salted water and boil until tender.

Meanwhile, to make the sauce, using a mortar and pestle, crush garlic with a little salt. Work in oil a drop at a time; as the sauce thickens the oil can be added more quickly. Season with salt and pepper.

Drain potatoes well. As soon as potatoes are cool enough to handle, cut into bite-size chunks and toss with sea salt and the sauce. Sprinkle with parsley and serve warm.

Makes 4 to 6 servings.

—POTATOES WITH RED SAUCE—

2 pounds walnut-size new potatoes, unpeeled
2 tablespoons sea salt
RED SAUCE:
4 large garlic cloves
Salt
1 teaspoon cumin seeds
1 teaspoon paprika
1/2 teaspoon dried leaf thyme
2/3 cup olive oil
2 teaspoons white-wine vinegar
3 tablespoons warm water

To make the sauce, using a mortar and pestle, crush garlic and a pinch of salt to a pulp.

Add cumin, paprika and thyme and crush well. Gradually mix in oil and vinegar, as making mayonnaise. Stir in warm water and set aside to cool completely.

In an uncovered saucepan, boil potatoes in just enough water to cover them. When most of water has evaporated, add the sea salt, which will form a crust on the potato skins. Allow water to boil away over low heat until it has all evaporated. Leave on heat about 30 seconds to dry potatoes thoroughly and produce a wrinkled effect; shake pan a little if potatoes start to burn. Serve in individual dishes accompanied by sauce.

Makes 4 servings.

—ROASTED VEGETABLE SALAD—

2 Spanish onions, unpeeled
1 pound small eggplants
2 red bell peppers
3 firm but ripe beefsteak tomatoes
8 garlic cloves
1-1/2 teaspoons cumin seeds
Juice of 1 lemon
1/4 cup extra-virgin olive oil
3 tablespoons white-wine vinegar
Salt
2 tablespoons finely chopped fresh parsley (optional)

Preheat oven to 350F (175C). Place onions on a baking sheet and bake 10 minutes. Add eggplants.

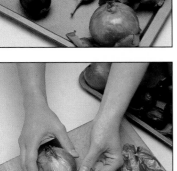

Bake another 10 minutes, then add peppers. Bake 10 minutes before adding tomatoes and 6 of the garlic cloves, then bake 15 minutes or until all vegetables are tender. If necessary, remove vegetables from oven as they are done. When vegetables are cool enough to handle, peel them with your fingers.

Remove and discard cores and seeds from peppers, then cut into strips. Halve tomatoes and discard seeds, then slice. Slice eggplants into strips and onions into rings. Arrange in a serving dish. Using a mortar and pestle, pound the roasted and the raw garlic and the cumin seeds to a paste. Beat in lemon juice, oil and vinegar. Add salt to taste. Pour over vegetables and sprinkle with parsley, if desired. Serve warm or cold.

Makes 4 servings.

──── ROASTED PEPPER SALAD ────

4 red bell peppers, roasted until charred (page 10)
4 canned anchovy fillets, drained and cut lengthwise
    into slivers
1 tablespoon capers, drained (optional)
1/2 cup extra-virgin olive oil
1 tablespoon finely chopped fresh parsley
Salt and black pepper

Peel peppers and remove and discard cores and seeds. Cut peppers into strips. In a shallow dish, place peppers. Arrange anchovy fillets on top and sprinkle with capers, if using.

In a small bowl, beat together oil, parsley, black pepper and just a little salt, if needed. Drizzle the dressing over peppers, anchovies and capers.

Makes 4 servings.

LEEK SALAD

8 long, slim leeks
1 small red bell pepper, cut into strips
1/2 cup extra-virgin olive oil
1/4 cup white-wine vinegar
Pinch of sugar
Large pinch of paprika
Salt and black pepper
Chopped parsley, capers (optional) and pitted oil-cured
    ripe olives, to garnish

In a saucepan of boiling salted water, cook leeks about 6 minutes or until tender but still firm.

Meanwhile, in a bowl, mix together bell pepper, oil, vinegar, sugar, paprika, salt and black pepper. Drain leeks well, pat dry with paper towels to absorb excess moisture, then place in a warm, shallow dish.

Pour vinegar mixture over leeks, turn leeks to coat well, then cover and let stand 2 hours in a cool place, turning leeks occasionally. Garnish with chopped fresh parsley, capers, if using, and ripe olives.

Makes 4 servings.

VEGETABLE SALAD

1 pound potatoes
1 large carrot, halved or quartered
1/3 cup shelled green peas
4 ounces green beans
2 tablespoons chopped Spanish onion
1 small red bell pepper, chopped
4 small pickles, chopped
1-1/2 tablespoons capers
8 to 12 anchovy-stuffed olives
2/3 cup mayonnaise
1 hard-cooked egg, sliced
Chopped fresh parsley, to garnish

In a saucepan of lightly salted water, boil potatoes in their skins until tender. Cool, peel, then dice. Boil carrot, peas and beans separately in boiling salted water until tender; drain and cool. Dice carrot and cut beans into short pieces.

Into a bowl, put potatoes, carrot, peas and beans. Stir in onion, pepper, pickles, capers, olives and mayonnaise while vegetables are still warm. Refrigerate until chilled. Arrange egg and chopped parsley on top before serving.

Makes 4 servings.

— WHITE SOUP WITH GRAPES —

7 ounces shelled almonds
4 slices day-old, firm white bread, crusts removed,
   soaked in cold water and squeezed dry
3 garlic cloves, finely crushed
1/2 cup olive oil
About 2-1/2 cups cold water
2 to 3 tablespoons sherry vinegar
Salt
1/2 pound muscat or other well-flavored grapes, peeled
   and seeded, if necessary
Chopped fresh parsley, to garnish

In a bowl, place almonds. Cover with boiling water. Leave 30 seconds, then remove nuts and squeeze them so they pop out of their skins. In a blender or food processor with the metal blade, combine nuts, bread and garlic. Process until smooth. With motor running, slowly pour in the oil. Add enough cold water to give a thin, creamy consistency.

Add vinegar and salt to taste. Add grapes, cover and refrigerate until chilled. Pour into a cold soup tureen or individual soup bowls. Serve garnished with chopped parsley.

Makes 4 to 6 servings.

GAZPACHO

1-1/2 pounds beefsteak tomatoes
1/2 Spanish onion, chopped
1 green bell pepper, chopped
1 red pepper, chopped
2 garlic cloves, chopped
2 slices firm white bread, crusts removed, broken into
    pieces
1-1/4 cups tomato juice
3 tablespoons extra-virgin olive oil
2 tablespoons sherry vinegar
Salt and black pepper
About 8 ice cubes, to serve
ACCOMPANIMENTS:
1 diced small red bell pepper, 1 diced small green bell
    pepper, 1 diced small onion, 1 chopped hard-cooked
    egg and croutons

With a sharp knife, peel, seed and chop tomatoes. In a blender or a food processor with the metal blade, combine tomatoes and remaining soup ingredients, except ice cubes. Process until smooth. Pour soup through a nylon strainer, pressing down well on contents of strainer. If necessary, thin soup with cold water, then cover and refrigerate until chilled.

Place accompaniments in separate bowls. Adjust seasoning of soup, if necessary, then pour into cold soup bowls. Add ice cubes and serve with accompaniments.

Makes 4 servings.

Variation: Do not strain the soup if more texture is preferred.

—LENTIL & CHORIZO SOUP—

3 cups (1 pound) green or brown lentils
1 Spanish onion, chopped
2 carrots, chopped
6 garlic cloves
6 to 8 ounces chorizo
4 bacon slices
1 bay leaf
2 beefsteak tomatoes, peeled, seeded and chopped
1 red bell pepper, chopped
1-1/2 tablespoons olive oil
1 Spanish onion, finely chopped
Salt and black pepper

Into a saucepan, put lentils, chopped onion, carrots, garlic, chorizo, pork, bay leaf, tomatoes and pepper. Just cover with water and bring to a boil. Cover and simmer about 30 minutes or until lentils are tender, pork is cooked and there is sufficient liquid left to make a thick soup.

Meanwhile, in a skillet, heat oil. Add finely chopped onion and cook over low heat about 15 minutes, stirring occasionally, until soft and lightly caramelized. Stir into lentils and season with salt and black pepper. Discard bay leaf. Slice chorizo and pork and return to lentils and heat through.

Makes 4 or 5 servings.

SPICY CHICKPEA SOUP

1-1/3 cups (8 ounces) chickpeas, soaked overnight, then drained
1/4 cup olive oil
1 slice bread, crusts removed
1 Spanish onion, finely chopped
8 ounces chorizo, thickly sliced
3 beefsteak tomatoes, peeled, seeded and chopped
1 tablespoon paprika
1/4 to 1/2 teaspoon cumin seeds, finely crushed
1 pound fresh spinach, chopped
3 garlic cloves

Cook chickpeas in 1-1/2 times their volume of boiling water 1-1/2 to 2 hours or until tender.

Meanwhile, in a small skillet, heat 2 tablespoons of the oil. Add bread and fry until golden on both sides. Remove and drain on paper towels. Add onion to pan and cook slowly, stirring occasionally, 5 minutes. Add chorizo and cook 5 to 10 minutes or until onion has softened but not colored. Stir tomatoes into onion and cook, stirring occasionally, about 10 minutes.

In a saucepan, heat remaining oil. Stir in paprika and cumin, then add spinach. Cook until spinach has wilted. Using a mortar and pestle, pound garlic with a pinch of salt. Add fried bread and pound again. Drain chickpeas, reserving liquid. Stir chickpeas into spinach with tomato and garlic mixtures and 3/4 cup chickpea liquid. Cover pan and simmer about 30 minutes; add more liquid if mixture becomes too dry.

Makes 4 servings.

—SCRAMBLED EGGS & SHRIMP—

2 tablespoons olive oil
3-1/2 cups sliced mixed brown, shiitake and oyster
    mushrooms (8 ounces)
1 to 2 tablespoons brandy
Salt and pepper
14 ounces raw shrimp, shelled
4 eggs, lightly beaten
2 tablespoons chopped fresh parsley
Fresh parsley, to garnish

In a wide skillet, heat oil. Add mushrooms.

Sprinkle brandy, salt and pepper over mush-rooms and cook over medium-high heat until the liquid has evaporated. Stir in shrimp and cook, stirring, 2 minutes.

Reduce heat to low, pour in eggs, add parsley and cook, stirring gently, until eggs are nearly set, but still creamy. Serve immediately on warm plates. Garnish with parsley.

Makes 2 to 3 servings.

EGGS FLAMENCA

2 tablespoons olive oil
1/2 Spanish onion, finely chopped
2 garlic cloves, crushed
4 slices serrano ham, chopped
1 small red bell pepper, finely chopped
Pinch paprika
1 large beefsteak tomato, peeled, seeded and chopped
3/4 cup fresh green peas or frozen peas, cooked
4 ounces green beans, cooked
1 teaspoon tomato paste (optional)
Salt and black pepper
4 eggs
4 slices chorizo
Fresh parsley, to garnish

Preheat oven to 450F (225C). In a skillet, heat oil. Add onion and garlic and cook about 4 minutes, stirring occasionally or until softened but not browned. Add 3/4 of the ham and bell pepper. Fry 2 minutes, then stir in paprika. Heat 1 minute. Add tomato. Simmer about 10 minutes or until reduced to a fairly thick puree. Add peas and beans and tomato paste if needed. Season with salt and black pepper.

Pour into a shallow baking dish, or 4 individual dishes. Form 4 shallow depressions in mixture. Carefully break eggs into depressions, allowing whites to flow over surface. Scatter remaining ham over the top and lay a chorizo slice on yolks. Bake 8 to 10 minutes or until egg whites are just set and yolks still moist. Bake 15 minutes if firmer eggs are preferred. Garnish with parsley and serve.

Makes 4 servings.

– ARTICHOKE & HAM TORTILLA –

3 artichokes
1/4 cup olive oil
2/3 cup finely diced serrano ham (4 ounces)
Salt and pepper
6 eggs, lightly beaten
Fresh parsley, to garnish

Trim artichokes to make artichoke bottoms (see page 50). Using a small sharp knife, cut each bottom into 8 pieces.

In a large skillet, heat oil. Add the artichoke pieces, ham and a little salt. Fry over low heat about 15 minutes, stirring occasionally, until artichoke pieces are just soft. Add pepper. Stir in eggs, spreading mixture evenly in pan. Cook over medium heat, shaking pan occasionally or until underside is set and beginning to brown.

Cover pan with a large plate and hold in place with one hand. Quickly turn pan upside down so omelet falls onto plate. Return pan to heat, add a little more oil, then slide omelet into pan, cooked side up. Cook until lightly browned underneath. Slide onto a serving plate. Serve warm or at room temperature. Garnish with parsley.

Makes 4 servings as a main course, or 8 as a tapa.

Note: Brown the omelet under the broiler instead of turning over, if preferred.

— TORTILLA WITH RED PEPPER —

6 tablespoons olive oil
1 pound potatoes, diced
1 Spanish onion, chopped
1 red bell pepper, chopped
5 eggs
1 tablespoon chopped fresh parsley
Salt and freshly ground black pepper

Heat oil in a large, heavy nonstick skillet. Add potatoes, onion and bell pepper to skillet. Cover and cook over low heat 15 to 20 minutes until soft but not brown, stirring occasionally to prevent sticking.

Drain off and reserve oil. In a bowl, lightly beat eggs. Mix in potatoes, onion and bell pepper and chopped parsley. Season with salt and black pepper. Let stand 10 minutes. Wipe skillet with paper towels. Add enough reserved oil to cover skillet bottom in a thin film. Add egg mixture, spreading it evenly in skillet. Cook over medium heat, shaking skillet occasionally, until underside is set and beginning to brown.

Cover skillet with a large plate and hold in place with one hand. Quickly turn skillet upside down so omelet falls onto plate. Return skillet to heat, add a little more oil, then slide omelet into skillet, cooked side up (see Note opposite). Cook until lightly browned on bottom. Slide onto a serving plate. Serve warm or at room temperature.

Makes 4 main-dish servings or 8 servings as a tapa.

— MONKFISH WITH PAPRIKA —

1-1/2 pounds skinned and filleted monkfish, cut into
   1-1/2-inch pieces
6 garlic cloves, crushed
1 tablespoon paprika
4 tablespoons olive oil
Salt and pepper
1/2 cup full-bodied dry white wine
Fresh chives and lemon wedges, to garnish

Into a bowl, put monkfish. In another small bowl, mix together garlic, paprika, 2 tablespoons oil, salt and pepper.

Pour mixture over fish; stir to coat the fish, then set aside 30 minutes.

In a skillet, heat remaining oil. Lift fish from bowl, add to pan and cook 2 to 3 minutes, stirring once or twice. Add any mixture remaining in bowl and the wine. Cook 5 to 7 minutes or until fish is no longer translucent in center. Serve garnished with chives and lemon wedges.

Makes 4 servings.

— MONKFISH & ALMOND SAUCE —

5 tablespoons olive oil
1/2 Spanish onion, chopped
2-1/4 pounds monkfish, skinned and cut into 8 pieces
Salt and pepper
2 garlic cloves, crushed
12 blanched almonds, toasted and finely ground
1 tablespoon chopped fresh parsley
Pinch of saffron threads, finely crushed
2 tablespoons dry white wine, fish stock or water
1-1/3 cups shelled fresh or frozen green peas (8 ounces)
Strips of lemon zest and fresh herbs, to garnish

In a large pan, heat 2 tablespoons of the oil. Add onion and cook 2 to 3 minutes. Season monkfish with salt and pepper and place on onion, add remaining oil and cook 5 minutes.

Meanwhile, using a mortar and pestle, pound garlic, almonds, parsley and saffron together to make a smooth paste. Stir in wine, stock or water. Add fresh peas and cook 7 to 10 minutes until fish is no longer translucent in center and peas are tender. If using frozen peas, add about 3 minutes before end of cooking time. Garnish with strips of lemon zest and fresh herbs.

Makes 4 servings.

— MONKFISH & ARTICHOKES —

1/4 cup white-wine vinegar
4 artichokes
2 tablespoons olive oil
1-1/2 pounds monkfish fillets, cut into 1-1/2-inch
    slices
Salt and pepper
1 small Spanish onion, finely chopped
4 garlic cloves, chopped
1 cup full-bodied dry white wine
2-1/2 pounds tomatoes
8 oil-cured ripe olives, pitted and halved
1 teaspoon capers
1 bay leaf
1 tablespoon chopped fresh parsley

Into a saucepan, pour 2 inches of water. Add vinegar. Break or cut off stem of 1 artichoke. Snap off and discard outer leaves, starting at bottom and continuing until pale yellow leaves are reached. Cut top two-thirds off artichoke. Using a small, sharp knife, pare off any dark green leaves that remain on the artichoke bottom. Cut the bottom into quarters; trim away any purple leaves and remove hairy choke. Cut each quarter into 4 pieces. Drop into pan.

Repeat with remaining artichokes, then simmer about 15 minutes or until tender. Drain and set aside.

In a skillet over high heat, heat oil. Add fish and sear on each side 1 minute. Transfer to a plate and season with salt and pepper. Add onion to pan, reduce heat to medium and cook onion about 4 minutes, stirring occasionally, or until softened but not colored. Stir in garlic, cook 1 minute, then add wine and boil until almost evaporated.

Stir in tomatoes, olives, capers, bay leaf and parsley. Boil about 10 minutes or until reduced by half.

Add artichokes and place monkfish on top. Reduce heat to medium, cover pan and cook until fish is no longer translucent in center, about 10 minutes. Transfer fish to a warm plate. Boil sauce to thicken slightly, adjust seasoning and pour over fish. Discard bay leaf.

Makes 4 servings.

—ROAST MONKFISH & GARLIC—

1 (2-1/4-lb.) monkfish tail, or 2 (1-lb.) pieces, skinned
2 garlic heads, divided into cloves
2 tablespoons olive oil
Salt and black pepper
1/4 teaspoon fresh thyme leaves
1/4 teaspoon fennel seeds
Juice of 1 lemon
1 bay leaf
1 large red bell pepper, cut into strips

Preheat oven to 425F (220C). Make sure membrane has been removed from fish. Cut out bone, then tie fish back into shape.

Using the point of a sharp knife, make some incisions in fish. Cut 2 garlic cloves into thin slices and push into incisions. In a skillet, heat 1 tablespoon of the oil. Add fish and brown on all sides, about 5 minutes. Remove and season with salt, black pepper, thyme, fennel and lemon juice.

Place fish on bay leaf in roasting pan. Arrange remaining garlic around fish. Bake 15 minutes. Add pepper strips and cook about 5 minutes or until fish is no longer translucent in center. Arrange fish, garlic, pepper and cooking juices on a plate. Carve fish in thin slices.

Makes 4 servings.

—SOLE WITH GREEN DRESSING—

Flour for coating
Salt and pepper
4 (6-oz.) sole or flounder fillets
1 egg, lightly beaten
About 1-1/2 cups fresh bread crumbs
1/4 cup olive oil
Lemon wedges and fresh herbs, to garnish
GREEN DRESSING:
3 garlic cloves
6 canned anchovy fillets, drained and chopped
3 tablespoons finely chopped fresh parsley
1/2 teaspoon chopped fresh oregano
1-1/2 tablespoons finely chopped capers
1-1/2 tablespoons fresh lemon juice
2/3 cup extra-virgin olive oil

To make the dressing, using a mortar and pestle, crush garlic with anchovies, then mix in parsley, oregano, capers and lemon juice. Beat in oil very slowly; set aside. Put flour on a plate and season with salt and pepper. Put egg and bread crumbs in separate shallow bowls. Coat fish in seasoned flour; dip in egg. Allow excess to drain off, then coat fish lightly and evenly in bread crumbs. Set aside 5 minutes.

In a large skillet, heat oil. Add fish and cook until golden and crisp, about 3 minutes each side. Cook fish in batches if necessary so pan is not crowded. Using a spatula, transfer fish to paper towels to drain. Garnish with lemon wedges and herbs. Stir dressing and serve with hot fish.

Makes 4 servings.

TROUT WITH HAM

4 trout, about 10 ounces each, cleaned
Salt and pepper
4 tablespoons olive oil
2/3 cup finely chopped serrano ham
2 garlic cloves, finely chopped
1 tablespoon chopped fresh parsley
Juice of 1 lemon
Parsley sprigs, to garnish

Season skin and inside cavities of each trout with salt and pepper.

In a large skillet, heat 2 tablespoons oil. Add trout and fry about 6 minutes or until trout just begins to flake when pierced with the point of a sharp knife. Transfer to a warm plate, cover and keep warm.

In a small saucepan, put remaining oil. Add ham and garlic and cook, stirring occasionally, until beginning to brown. Stir in parsley and lemon juice and heat a few minutes. Pour the mixture over the trout. Serve garnished with parsley sprigs.

Makes 4 servings.

MULLET WITH ANCHOVY SAUCE

4 red mullet, about 8 ounces each, scaled and cleaned
8 canned anchovy fillets, drained and rinsed
Flour for coating
Salt and pepper
Olive oil
1/2 cup freshly squeezed orange juice
4 tablespoons peeled, seeded and chopped tomato
Chopped fresh parsley, capers and orange sections, to
    garnish

Preheat broiler. Using the point of a sharp knife, cut 2 diagonal slashes in both sides of each fish. Cut 4 anchovy fillets into 4 pieces and insert 1 piece in each slash. Roughly chop remaining anchovy fillets. Season flour with salt and pepper, then coat fish lightly and evenly.

Brush fish with oil, then place under very hot broiler until crisp and fish just begins to flake when pierced with a knife, about 5 minutes each side. Transfer to a warm serving plate and keep warm. Stir orange juice, tomato and chopped anchovies into juices in broiler pan, then pour into a saucepan. Place over direct heat and boil until thickened to a light sauce. Season with pepper. Pour sauce around fish and garnish with parsley, capers and orange sections.

Makes 4 servings.

—HALIBUT IN WINE SAUCE—

4 tablespoons olive oil
Flour for coating
Salt and pepper
2 pounds halibut, cut into 1-inch-thick slices
1/2 Spanish onion, finely chopped
2 canned anchovy fillets, drained and coarsely chopped
3 tablespoons chopped fresh parsley
3/4 cup dry white wine
Squeeze of lemon juice

In a large skillet, heat 3 tablespoons of the oil. Season flour with salt and pepper. Coat fish evenly in the seasoned flour. Add fish slices to pan, making sure they are not crowded. Cook 5 minutes on each side.

Meanwhile, in a small saucepan, heat remaining oil. Add onion and cook over low heat about 7 minutes until lightly colored. Add anchovies and parsley and cook, stirring and mashing anchovies with a wooden spoon, until anchovies are blended in. Stir in wine and boil until reduced by half. Add pepper and lemon juice to taste. Spoon or pour surplus oil from skillet; pour sauce over the fish. Cook over medium heat 2 minutes, basting occasionally. Serve.

Makes 4 servings.

– HAKE WITH PEAS & POTATOES –

1/2 Spanish onion, thinly sliced
8 garlic cloves, sliced
4 potatoes, thinly sliced
3 fresh parsley sprigs
1 bay leaf
Salt
4 hake steaks, about 1/2 pound each
1-1/3 cups shelled fresh or frozen green peas (8 ounces)
6 tablespoons olive oil
1 tablespoon paprika

In a heavy pan, put onion, 2 garlic cloves, the potatoes, parsley and bay leaf.

Just cover with cold water. Add salt and simmer 10 minutes. Add hake and fresh peas and simmer about 10 minutes or until vegetables are tender and fish just begins to flake. If using frozen peas, add about 3 minutes before the end of cooking time. Strain off excess cooking liquid.

Meanwhile, in a small skillet, heat oil. Add remaining garlic and fry 4 to 5 minutes until lightly colored. Remove from heat and sprinkle in paprika. Stir quickly and pour over fish, potatoes and peas. Serve immediately.

Makes 4 servings.

— COD WITH PARSLEY CRUST —

1-1/2 pounds cod, haddock or hake fillets, skinned
Salt and pepper
2 garlic cloves, crushed
1/3 cup olive oil
1 cup fresh bread crumbs
2 tablespoons chopped fresh parsley
1/4 cup fresh lemon juice
Parsley and lime wedges, to garnish

Season fish with salt and pepper and put in a shallow baking dish.

In a bowl, mix together garlic and 4 tablespoons of the oil. Pour over fish, cover and refrigerate 1 hour. Meanwhile, preheat oven to 350F (175C).

In a bowl, mix together bread crumbs, parsley and lemon juice. Sprinkle evenly over fish, then drizzle with remaining olive oil. Bake about 15 minutes or until fish just begins to flake when tested with point of a sharp knife. Serve hot, garnished with parsley and lime wedges.

Makes 4 servings.

FISH IN GREEN SAUCE

3 tablespoons olive oil
4 hake or cod steaks, about 6 ounces each
1/2 Spanish onion, finely chopped
3 garlic cloves, chopped
1/2 cup fish stock
2 tablespoons chopped fresh parsley
3/4 cup slivered, toasted almonds
Salt and pepper
Fennel sprigs, to garnish

In a skillet, heat oil. Add fish and cook 2 minutes on each side.

Using a spatula, transfer fish to a warmed plate, cover and keep warm. Add onion to oil remaining in pan and fry 3 minutes. Stir in garlic and fry 3 minutes, then stir in stock, parsley and almonds. Simmer about 3 minutes or until slightly thickened.

Transfer almond mixture to a blender or food processor with the metal blade and process until smooth. Season with salt and pepper. Return fish to pan, pour the sauce over the top and heat through 1 to 2 minutes. Garnish with fennel.

Makes 4 servings.

—— COD & EGGPLANT STEW ——

1 eggplant, cubed
Salt and pepper
1-1/2 pounds thick cod fillets, cut into 4 pieces
5 ounces cured chorizo, skinned and thinly sliced
1/4 cup olive oil
1 Spanish onion, finely chopped
2 garlic cloves, very finely chopped
1 red bell pepper, cut into strips
3 cups peeled, seeded and chopped beefsteak tomatoes
1/2 cup dry white wine
Chopped fresh parsley, to garnish

Into a colander, place eggplant. Sprinkle with salt and leave 30 minutes. Rinse well and dry with paper towels. Halve each piece of cod horizontally without cutting completely in half. Open out like a book. Lay a quarter of the chorizo on 1 side of each piece, then cover with other side. In a large pan, heat oil. Add fish and cook until evenly browned. Using a spatula, remove fish from pan and set aside.

Add onion to pan and cook over low heat, about 7 minutes, stirring occasionally or until soft but not colored. Stir in garlic, eggplant and bell pepper. Cook about 4 minutes, then add tomatoes and wine and simmer about 20 minutes or until vegetables are tender. Season tomato mixture and return fish to pan. Cook 10 minutes. Garnish with parsley.

Makes 4 servings.

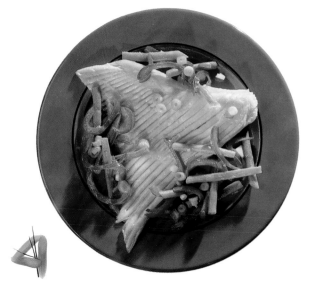

——— SKATE WITH RED PEPPER ———

2 pounds skate wings, skinned
Salt and black pepper
2 cups dry white wine
1 cup fish stock or water
2 tablespoons chopped Spanish onion
2 fresh thyme sprigs
8 whole cloves
4 green onions, thinly sliced
1/4 cup mild red-wine vinegar
2 tablespoons extra-virgin olive oil
1 tablespoon fresh lemon juice
1 red bell pepper, thinly sliced
5 ounces green beans, halved diagonally lengthwise

Rinse skate under cold running water, then season with salt and black pepper. In a large skillet, bring wine, stock or water, onion, thyme and cloves to a boil. Reduce heat, add skate and poach about 12 minutes or until skate changes from translucent to opaque. Meanwhile, in a bowl, mix together green onions, vinegar, oil and lemon juice. Set aside. Using a spatula, transfer cooked skate to a warm plate and cover to keep warm.

Strain cooking liquid, then return it to pan and season with salt and black pepper. Add bell pepper. Simmer 5 minutes. Add beans and cook 5 minutes. Using a slotted spoon, transfer vegetables to a bowl. Boil liquid in pan about 3 minutes or until lightly syrupy, then pour into bowl of green onions. Lift skate flesh from cartilage and place on a serving plate. Arrange vegetables around fish and spoon the green onions and liquid over the top. Serve warm or cold.

Makes 4 servings.

ZARZUELA

16 mussels
12 ounces squid
3 tablespoons olive oil
1 pound raw shrimp in their shells
1-1/4 pounds monkfish, cut into 4 slices
Salt and pepper
1/4 cup Spanish brandy
1 large Spanish onion, finely chopped
1 teaspoon paprika
2 beefsteak tomatoes, peeled, seeded and chopped
1 bay leaf
1/2 cup dry white wine
1/2 cup fish stock
3 saffron threads, crushed
3 garlic cloves
3 tablespoons chopped fresh parsley

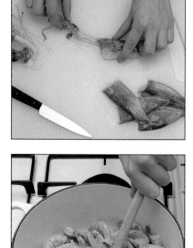

Clean and cook mussels (page 12), remove from shells and set aside. Clean squid (page 17), chop tentacles and slice bodies into rings; set aside.

In a large pan, heat oil. Add shrimp and fry until pink. Transfer to a plate. Season monkfish, add to oil and fry over medium heat until light brown. Add squid rings and tentacles and fry briefly. Pour in brandy and warm, then ignite. When flames die down, tip contents of pan into a bowl and set aside.

Add onion to pan and cook over low heat about 4 minutes or until soft. Stir in paprika and cook 30 to 60 seconds.

Add tomatoes and bay leaf and simmer 2 to 3 minutes. Stir in wine and boil until reduced by one-third. Stir in stock and simmer 3 to 4 minutes.

Pound saffron, garlic and parsley together with a mortar and pestle, mix in a little hot stock, then return to pan. Boil 1 minute. Add contents of bowl, the mussels and shrimp and simmer about 5 minutes.

Makes 4 servings.

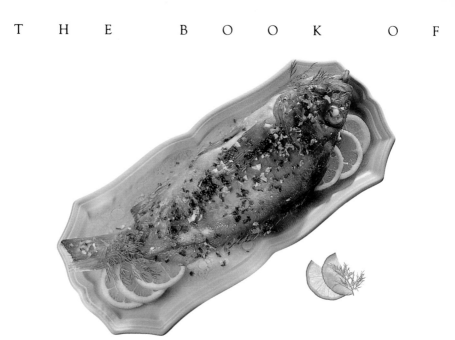

─── BAKED SEA BREAM ───

2 sea bream, about 2 pounds each, cleaned
Salt and pepper
4 garlic cloves, crushed
2 fresh parsley sprigs, chopped
1/4 cup olive oil
Juice of 1 lemon
3/4 cup dry white wine
Fennel and lemon slices, to garnish

Preheat oven to 375F (190C). Season fish inside and out with salt and pepper.

Into a shallow baking dish, put fish. Scatter garlic and parsley over fish. Pour olive oil, lemon juice and wine over fish.

Bake fish about 20 minutes or until fish just begins to flake when pierced with a knife. Serve garnished with fennel and lemon slices.

Makes 4 servings.

——CHICKEN WITH PARSLEY——

3 tablespoons olive oil
1 (3-1/2-lb.) chicken, cut into 8 pieces
3 garlic cloves, lightly crushed
1/2 fresh red chile, seeded and finely chopped
6 tablespoons dry white wine
Salt and pepper
Juice of 1/2 lemon
3 tablespoons chopped fresh parsley

In a large pan, heat oil. Add chicken and cook about 10 minutes or until lightly browned. Cook in batches, if necessary. Remove and reserve.

Add garlic and chile to pan and cook 5 minutes without browning, stirring occasionally. Return chicken to pan, add wine and boil 2 to 3 minutes.

Season lightly, cover and cook about 40 minutes or until chicken juices run clear when chicken is pierced with a sharp knife. Transfer chicken to a warm plate and keep warm. Stir lemon juice and parsley into pan. Boil if necessary to reduce juices, then pour over chicken.

Makes 4 servings.

Variation: Use 4 large chicken portions, halved, instead of whole chicken.

-CHICKEN IN SANFAINA SAUCE-

1/4 cup olive oil
1 (3-lb.) chicken, cut into 8 pieces
2 Spanish onions, chopped
2 garlic cloves, chopped
1 green bell pepper, sliced
1 red bell pepper, sliced
2 eggplants, cut into strips
4 ounces serrano ham, diced
1 pound beefsteak tomatoes, peeled, seeded and
  chopped
1/2 cup dry white wine
1/2 cup chicken stock
Bouquet garni of 1 bay leaf, 1 thyme sprig and 1 parsley
  sprig
Salt and pepper
1 tablespoon chopped fresh parsley, to garnish

In a large, heavy pan, heat oil, add chicken and fry until lightly browned, about 10 minutes. Using a slotted spoon, remove chicken and reserve. Add onions and garlic to pan and fry 1 minute. Add peppers and eggplants and cook, stirring occasionally, 5 minutes. Stir in ham, tomatoes, wine, stock, bouquet garni, salt and pepper.

Bring mixture to a boil, then reduce heat so liquid barely simmers. Return chicken to pan, spooning sauce over it. Cover pan and simmer about 45 minutes until chicken juices run clear when chicken is pierced with sharp knife, and sauce is slightly thickened. Discard bouquet garni. Taste and adjust the seasoning. Serve sprinkled with parsley.

Makes 4 servings.

Variation: Use 4 large chicken portions, halved, instead of whole chicken.

———— CHICKEN WITH SHERRY ————

1/4 cup raisins
1 cup oloroso sherry
3 tablespoons olive oil
1 (3-1/2-lb.) chicken, cut into 8 pieces (see page 66)
1 Spanish onion, finely chopped
1 garlic clove, finely chopped
1 cup chicken stock
Salt and pepper
4 tablespoons pine nuts

In a small bowl, soak raisins in sherry 30 minutes.

In a large pan, heat 2 tablespoons of the oil, add chicken and cook until lightly and evenly browned, about 10 minutes. Transfer to paper towels to drain. Add onion and garlic to pan and cook over low heat, stirring occasionally, until softened and lightly colored, about 7 minutes. Strain raisins, reserving sherry, and set aside.

Stir sherry into pan. Simmer until reduced by half. Add stock, chicken, salt and pepper, bring to a boil, then reduce heat and simmer until chicken is tender, about 35 minutes. In a small pan, heat remaining oil. Add pine nuts and cook until lightly colored. Drain on paper towels, then stir into pan with raisins. Transfer chicken to a warm serving dish. Boil liquid in pan to reduce slightly. Pour over chicken.

Makes 4 servings.

SPICY CHICKEN

1/4 cup olive oil
4 slices day-old French bread
8 garlic cloves
1 (3-1/2-lb.) chicken, skinned and cut into small pieces
1-1/4 cups medium-bodied dry white wine
Large pinch saffron threads, finely crushed
3 tablespoons chopped fresh parsley
3 whole cloves
Freshly grated nutmeg
Salt and pepper

In a large pan, heat oil. Add bread and 5 garlic cloves and fry until lightly browned. Break into pieces.

Using a mortar and pestle, crush cooked garlic and bread, then add remaining garlic and crush. Add to pan with chicken. Cook until chicken changes color. Pour in wine and just enough water to cover chicken. Cover pan and simmer about 30 minutes or until chicken juices run clear when thickest part is pierced with a sharp knife.

Meanwhile, in a bowl, dissolve saffron in 2 tablespoons of the chicken cooking liquid. Put parsley, cloves and nutmeg in the mortar and pound to a paste. Stir in the saffron. Mix with crushed bread, then stir the mixture into the pan and cook 10 minutes. Season to taste with salt and pepper and serve.

Makes 4 servings.

CHICKEN WITH WALNUT SAUCE

6 chicken breast halves
Salt and pepper
Juice of 1 orange
1-1/4 cups walnut halves
2 garlic cloves, chopped
2 tablespoons water
1/3 cup walnut oil
1/3 cup olive oil
Squeeze of lemon juice
Chopped fresh parsley and orange slices, to serve

Preheat oven to 400F (205C). Season chicken breast halves with salt and pepper and place in a large shallow bowl. Pour orange juice over chicken; set aside.

On a baking sheet, spread out walnuts. Bake until lightly browned, 5 to 10 minutes. Transfer to a blender or food processor with the metal blade. Add garlic, water and a pinch of salt. Process to a paste. With motor running, slowly pour in walnut and olive oils to make a smooth, mayonnaise-like sauce. Transfer to a bowl; add lemon juice and pepper to taste; set aside.

Preheat broiler. Broil chicken 5 to 7 minutes on each side until juices run clear when thickest part is pierced with a sharp knife. Sprinkle orange slices with chopped parsley; use to garnish chicken, then serve with the sauce.

Makes 6 servings.

— CHICKEN IN VINEGAR SAUCE —

4 boneless chicken breast halves
Salt and pepper
1/3 cup olive oil
12 garlic cloves
1 small onion, finely chopped
About 3 tablespoons sherry vinegar
1 tablespoon paprika
1-1/2 tablespoons chopped fresh oregano
2 tablespoons fresh bread crumbs
1-1/4 cups chicken stock
Fresh herbs, to garnish

Season chicken with salt and pepper. In a heavy pan, heat oil. Add chicken and cook 10 minutes.

Meanwhile, slice 4 of the garlic cloves. Add sliced garlic to pan with the onion and cook about 5 minutes or until chicken is lightly browned all over.

Remove chicken from pan, stir in vinegar and boil 2 to 3 minutes. Return chicken to pan. Pound remaining garlic with a little salt, the paprika and oregano, then stir in bread crumbs and a quarter of the stock. Pour over chicken, add remaining stock and cook about 20 minutes or until chicken is tender and sauce is fairly thick. Adjust seasoning and amount of vinegar, if necessary. Serve garnished with fresh herbs.

Makes 4 servings.

CHICKEN PEPITORIA

2 tablespoons olive oil
1 (3-1/2-lb.) chicken, cut into 8 pieces, or 4 large
   chicken portions, halved
1/2 Spanish onion, finely chopped
4 ounces serrano ham, cut into strips
1 cup chicken stock
4 garlic cloves, crushed
15 almonds or hazelnuts, lightly toasted
Pinch of ground cloves
3 tablespoons chopped fresh parsley
3 egg yolks
Salt and pepper
Fresh parsley, to garnish

In a large pan, heat oil. Add chicken and fry until lightly browned all over. Using a slotted spoon, remove chicken from pan and set aside. Add onion to pan and cook about 4 minutes, stirring occasionally. Stir in ham and cook 1 minute, then return chicken to pan. Pour in the stock, cover tightly and simmer about 45 minutes or until chicken is tender.

Meanwhile, using a mortar and pestle, pound together garlic, nuts, cloves and parsley. Place in a small bowl and gradually work in egg yolks. Stir a little hot chicken liquid into the bowl, then stir mixture into the pan. Simmer, stirring, until sauce thickens; do not boil or sauce may curdle. Season with salt and pepper. Garnish with parsley.

Makes 4 servings.

-CHICKEN WITH GARLIC SAUCE-

4 chicken portions
Salt and pepper
6 tablespoons olive oil
3 tablespoons fresh lemon juice
2 tablespoons finely chopped green onions
2 tablespoons chopped fresh parsley
1 recipe Garlic Sauce (page 34)
2 lemons, quartered

Rub chicken with salt and pepper, then place in a single layer in a non-metallic dish.

Pour oil and lemon juice over the chicken and let stand 1 hour, turning chicken over once or twice.

Preheat broiler. Place chicken on a broiler rack and broil slowly 8 to 10 minutes on each side, basting occasionally with the oil and lemon mixture, until crisp on the outside and tender throughout. Transfer to a warm serving plate and sprinkle onions and parsley over the top. Serve with Garlic Sauce and lemon quarters.

Makes 4 servings.

QUAIL WITH GRAPES

3 tablespoons olive oil
1 Spanish onion, finely chopped
2 small carrots, finely chopped
Salt and pepper
8 bacon slices
8 quail
4 black peppercorns
2 garlic cloves
9 ounces muscatel grapes, peeled and seeded
Pinch of freshly grated nutmeg
1 cup medium-bodied dry white wine
1/4 cup Spanish brandy

Preheat oven to 375F (190C). In a heavy roasting pan that will hold the quail in a single layer, heat oil. Add onion and carrots and cook, stirring occasionally, 4 to 5 minutes. Season quail inside and out, lay a slice of bacon over each one and tie in place with string. Place on the vegetables, then roast 30 minutes.

Meanwhile, using a mortar and pestle, crush peppercorns and garlic, then work in half the grapes, the nutmeg, wine and brandy. Pour mixture over quail and cook 30 minutes, basting occasionally. Add remaining grapes, then transfer quail, vegetables and grapes to a warm serving plate; keep warm. Carefully pour cooking liquid into a saucepan. Boil liquid until lightly thickened. Season with salt and pepper. Pour sauce over quail.

Makes 4 to 6 servings.

SPANISH PARTRIDGES

2 partridges, cut in half lengthwise
2 tablespoons brandy
Salt and pepper
3 tablespoons olive oil
1 Spanish onion, chopped
3 garlic cloves, finely chopped
2 tablespoons all-purpose flour
1/4 cup red-wine vinegar
1 cup red wine
1 cup chicken stock
6 black peppercorns
2 whole cloves
1 bay leaf
2 carrots, cut into short lengths
8 shallots
1 ounce chocolate, grated

Rub partridges with brandy, salt and pepper and set aside 30 minutes. In a heavy pan into which the birds fit snugly, heat oil. Add onion and cook, stirring occasionally, 3 minutes. Stir in garlic and cook 2 minutes.

Sprinkle birds lightly with flour, then fry in pan 5 minutes on each side. Remove and set aside.

Stir vinegar into pan and boil 1 to 2 minutes. Add wine and boil 1 to 2 minutes, then add stock, peppercorns, cloves, bay leaf and partridges. Heat to a simmer, cover tightly and simmer 40 minutes. Add carrots and shallots, cover again and simmer 20 minutes.

Transfer partridges, shallots and carrots to a warm dish. If necessary, boil the cooking juices until reduced to 1-1/4 cups, then puree in a blender or food processor with the metal blade.

Return juices to pan over low heat and stir in chocolate until melted. Return partridges and vegetables to pan and turn them over in the sauce to coat.

Makes 4 servings.

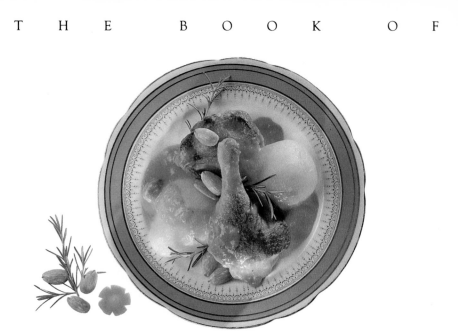

— DUCK WITH PEARS —

2 tablespoons olive oil
1 (4-1/2-lb.) duck, cut into 8 serving pieces
2 Spanish onions, finely chopped
1 carrot, chopped
2 beefsteak tomatoes, peeled, seeded and chopped
1 cinnamon stick
1 teaspoon chopped fresh thyme
1 cup chicken stock
1/4 cup Spanish brandy
14 firm pears, peeled, cored and halved
1 garlic clove
10 almonds, toasted
Salt and pepper
Fresh herbs, to garnish

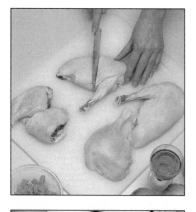

In a skillet, heat oil. Add duck in batches, skin-side down, and cook over medium-high heat about 10 minutes or until browned. Turn over and cook about 8 minutes or until underside is lightly browned. Using tongs, transfer duck to paper towels to drain.

Remove excess oil from pan, leaving about 2 tablespoons. Add onions, carrot, tomatoes, cinnamon and thyme and cook about 5 minutes, stirring occasionally, until onions have softened but not browned. Add stock and simmer 20 minutes.

Discard cinnamon, then puree contents of pan in a blender or food processor with the metal blade, or rub through a strainer. Return to pan, add brandy and boil 1 to 2 minutes. Add duck and heat through 5 to 10 minutes.

Meanwhile, into a saucepan into which the pears just fit, put pears. Just cover pears with water and simmer until tender.

Using a mortar and pestle, pound garlic and almonds to a paste. Mix in a little of the pear cooking liquid, then stir into brandy sauce. Thin sauce, if necessary, with more pear cooking liquid. Season to taste with salt and pepper. Transfer duck to a warmed serving plate and pour the sauce over the top. Arrange pears around duck. Garnish with herbs.

Makes 4 servings.

DUCK & OLIVES

3 tablespoons olive oil
1 (4-1/2-lb.) duck, cut into 4 pieces
1 Spanish onion, finely chopped
1 tablespoon all-purpose flour
2 beefsteak tomatoes, peeled, seeded and chopped
3/4 cup dry white wine
3 tablespoons water
4 bay leaves
3 fresh parsley sprigs
3 garlic cloves, crushed
Salt and pepper
8 ounces green olives
Fresh herbs, to garnish

In a large pan, heat half the oil. Add duck in batches, brown evenly, then transfer to paper towels to drain. Heat remaining oil in pan, add onion and cook 6 to 8 minutes, stirring occasionally, until golden and translucent. Stir in flour, then tomatoes, wine, water, bay leaves, parsley and garlic. Season with salt and pepper. Bring to a boil, stirring. Add duck pieces, reduce heat, cover and simmer 30 minutes.

Into a bowl, put olives. Cover with boiling water, then drain well. Add to pan, cover tightly and cook about 30 minutes or until juices run clear when thickest part of duck is pierced with a skewer. Skim excess fat from surface, and adjust seasoning, if necessary. Garnish with herbs.

Makes 4 servings.

LAMB CHILINDRON

1/4 cup olive oil
1-1/2 pounds lean lamb, cubed
Salt and black pepper
1 Spanish onion, chopped
2 garlic cloves, chopped
3 red bell peppers, cut into strips
4 beefsteak tomatoes, peeled, seeded and chopped
1 dried red chile, chopped
Chopped fresh herbs, to garnish

In a large pan, heat oil. Season lamb with salt and black pepper and add to pan.

Cook, stirring, until evenly browned, then using a slotted spoon, transfer to a bowl. Add onion to pan and cook about 4 minutes, stirring occasionally, until softened but not colored. Stir in garlic, cook 1 to 2 minutes, then stir in peppers, tomatoes and chile. Simmer 5 minutes.

Return lamb and any juices that have collected in bowl to pan. Cover tightly and simmer about 1-1/2 hours, or until lamb is tender. Taste for seasoning and adjust if necessary. Serve garnished with chopped herbs.

Makes 6 servings.

——— LAMB WITH RIPE OLIVES ———

1/4 cup olive oil
1-1/2 pounds lean lamb, cut into small cubes
1 (4-oz.) piece unsmoked bacon, cut into small strips
2 garlic cloves, sliced
1/2 to 1 teaspoon chopped fresh oregano
3/4 cup full-bodied white wine
1 fresh red chile, seeded and finely chopped
12 to 15 ripe olives, pitted
Fresh herbs, to garnish

In a wide, shallow pan, heat oil. Add lamb, pork and garlic and cook over high heat to seal and brown meat.

In a small saucepan, boil oregano and wine 2 to 3 minutes. Stir into pan, cover and simmer 30 minutes.

Stir chile and olives into pan. Cover again and cook about 30 minutes or until lamb is tender. If necessary, uncover pan toward end of cooking time so liquid can evaporate to make a thin sauce. Garnish with herbs.

Makes 4 servings.

——————— SPICE-COATED LAMB ———————

4 garlic cloves
1/4 teaspoon cumin seeds
1 tablespoon paprika
1/4 teaspoon saffron threads, crushed
Salt and pepper
1-1/2 pounds lean lamb, cut into 1 to 1-1/2-inch cubes
3 tablespoons olive oil
2/3 cup full-bodied dry white wine

Using a mortar and pestle, pound together garlic, cumin, paprika, saffron, salt and pepper.

Into a bowl, put lamb. Add spice mixture and stir well but gently to coat lamb. Set aside 30 minutes.

In a large pan, heat oil. Add lamb and cook 5 to 6 minutes, stirring occasionally, until lamb has browned. Stir in wine and heat to a simmer. Cover tightly and simmer 30 to 40 minutes or until meat is tender and sauce thickened.

Makes 4 servings.

LAMB IN HERB SAUCE

2 tablespoons olive oil
1-1/2 pounds lean boneless lamb, cut into pieces
1 Spanish onion, chopped
2 green bell peppers, chopped
3 garlic cloves, crushed
3/4 cup dry white wine
2/3 cup water
1-1/2 teaspoons chopped fresh thyme
Salt and pepper
1 small head lettuce, sliced
2 tablespoons chopped fresh parsley
2 tablespoons chopped fresh mint
2 ounces pine nuts
Mint sprigs and pine nuts, to garnish

In a large pan, heat oil. Add lamb and fry, stirring occasionally, until evenly browned. Using a slotted spoon, remove lamb and set aside. Stir onion into pan and cook about 4 minutes, stirring occasionally, until softened but not browned. Stir in bell pepper and garlic and cook 2 to 3 minutes, then stir in wine. Boil 1 minute.

Pour in water and bring to a boil. Reduce heat so liquid just simmers, then add lamb, thyme, salt and pepper. Cover and simmer about 1 hour. Stir in lettuce, parsley, mint and pine nuts, cover and cook 10 to 15 minutes. Serve garnished with mint sprigs and pine nuts.

Makes 4 servings.

–LAMB WITH LEMON & GARLIC–

3 tablespoons olive oil
2 pounds lean, boneless lamb, cut into 1-inch pieces
1 Spanish onion, finely chopped
3 garlic cloves, crushed
1 tablespoon paprika
3 tablespoons finely chopped fresh parsley
3 tablespoons fresh lemon juice
Salt and pepper
3 tablespoons dry white wine (optional)

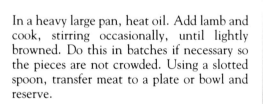

In a heavy large pan, heat oil. Add lamb and cook, stirring occasionally, until lightly browned. Do this in batches if necessary so the pieces are not crowded. Using a slotted spoon, transfer meat to a plate or bowl and reserve.

Stir onion into pan and cook about 5 minutes, stirring occasionally, until softened. Stir in garlic and cook 2 minutes, then stir in paprika. When well blended, stir in lamb and any juices on plate or in bowl, the parsley, lemon juice, salt and pepper. Cover tightly and cook over very low heat 1-1/4 to 1-1/2 hours, shaking pan occasionally, until lamb is very tender. If necessary, add wine or 3 tablespoons water.

Makes 4 to 6 servings.

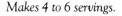

– BRAISED LAMB & VEGETABLES –

1 pound firm, yellow potatoes, cut into 1/4-inch slices
2 garlic cloves, pounded to a paste
6 to 8 green onions, thinly sliced
2 medium or large artichoke bottoms (page 50), sliced
3 cups chopped brown mushrooms
Handful of parsley, finely chopped
1 tablespoon chopped mixed herbs
Salt and pepper
3 tablespoons olive oil
4 lamb shoulder or loin chops
3/4 cup full-bodied dry white wine
Fresh parsley sprigs, to garnish

Preheat oven to 375F (190C). In a bowl, combine potatoes, garlic, green onions, artichoke bottoms, mushrooms, parsley, mixed herbs, salt and pepper. In a heavy large pan, heat half the mixture. In a skillet, heat oil. Add lamb and brown on both sides. Drain on paper towels, then season with salt and pepper and place in pan.

Over the heat, stir wine into skillet to dislodge cooking juices, bring to a boil and pour over the lamb. Cover with remaining vegetables and add enough water to almost cover vegetables. Bring to a boil. Cover and cook in the oven about 30 minutes. Uncover and cook 1 hour or until lamb is tender. Add a little water if it seems too dry. Garnish with parsley.

Makes 4 servings.

——— BEEF IN SPINACH SAUCE ———

2 tablespoons olive oil
1-1/2 pounds beef chuck steak, cut into 1-1/2-inch
  cubes
8 pearl onions
1 tablespoon red-wine vinegar
8 ounces fresh spinach, trimmed
1 tablespoon fresh bread crumbs
3 garlic cloves
About 2 cups veal stock or water
Salt and pepper
1 tablespoon ripe olive paste

In a large pan, heat oil. Add beef and brown on all sides. Remove with a slotted spoon and set aside. Add onions to pan and cook, stirring frequently, until evenly browned. Stir in vinegar and boil 1 minute.

Into a blender or food processor with the metal blade, put spinach, bread crumbs, garlic and half the stock or water. Process until smooth. Return beef to pan, add spinach mixture and remaining stock or water. Season with salt and pepper. Heat to a simmer, then cover and simmer over very low heat 1-1/2 to 2 hours until beef is tender. Stir in olive paste and serve.

Makes 4 to 6 servings.

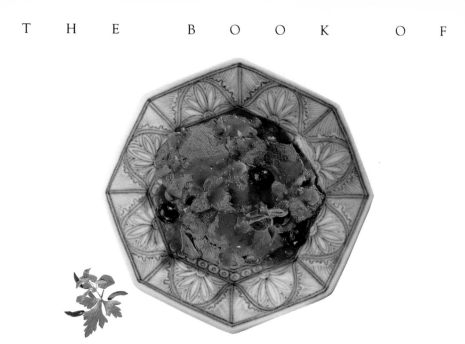

—BEEF WITH TOMATO SAUCE—

2 garlic cloves, thinly sliced
1 tablespoon finely chopped fresh thyme
1 tablespoon finely chopped fresh marjoram
1 (1-1/2-lb.) beef chuck steak
2 tablespoons olive oil
TOMATO SAUCE:
2 tablespoons olive oil
8 garlic cloves, chopped
1 fresh thyme sprig
2 fresh marjoram sprigs
3 fresh parsley sprigs
1 (14-oz) can chopped tomatoes
8 canned anchovy fillets, drained and chopped
3/4 cup dry white wine
24 small ripe olives, pitted
Salt and pepper

To make the sauce, in a saucepan, heat oil. Add garlic and herbs and simmer 5 minutes. Add tomatoes with their juice, then stir in anchovies, wine and olives. Simmer 15 minutes. Season to taste with salt and pepper.

Meanwhile, mix garlic with chopped herbs. Using the point of a sharp knife, cut small slits in beef and push the herb-covered slices of garlic deep into slits. In a large pan, heat oil. Add beef and cook 10 minutes until evenly browned. Add sauce, cover tightly and simmer about 1-1/2 hours, turning beef occasionally, until beef is tender.

Makes 4 servings.

GARLIC BEEF

2 tablespoons olive oil
1 (4-oz) piece slab bacon, cut into 2-inch cubes
1 (2-lb.) beef chuck steak, cut into 1-1/2-inch cubes
1 Spanish onion, chopped
1 head garlic, divided into cloves
1 cup red wine
2 whole cloves
Bouquet garni of 1 fresh marjoram sprig, 1 fresh thyme
    sprig, 2 fresh parsley sprigs and 1 bay leaf
Salt and pepper

In a large pan, heat oil. Add bacon and cook over low heat until bacon is almost crisp. Increase heat, add beef and cook about 5 minutes, stirring occasionally, until browned all over. Using a slotted spoon, transfer beef and bacon to a bowl.

Stir onion and garlic into pan and cook 6 minutes, stirring occasionally. Stir in wine, cloves, bouquet garni, salt and pepper. Return meat to pan, cover tightly and simmer 2 hours, stirring occasionally, until meat is very tender. Add a little water if mixture gets too dry. Discard bouquet garni.

Makes 6 servings.

——— PORK WITH HERB SAUCE ———

1/2 cup fresh white bread crumbs
2 tablespoons white-wine vinegar
2 garlic cloves
2 canned anchovy fillets, drained
1/4 cup chopped fresh parsley
2 teaspoons capers, drained
1 hard-cooked egg yolk
1 cup extra-virgin olive oil
Salt and pepper
4 boneless pork loin chops, about 1 inch thick

In a small bowl, soak bread crumbs in vinegar.

Meanwhile, using a mortar and pestle, crush garlic with anchovy fillets, parsley, capers and egg yolk. Squeeze vinegar from bread crumbs, then mix bread crumbs into mortar. Slowly stir in oil to make a creamy sauce. Add salt and pepper to taste. Set aside.

Preheat broiler. Broil chops about 12 minutes on each side until lightly browned and cooked through but still juicy in center. Season chops with salt and pepper and top with some of sauce. Serve remaining sauce separately.

Makes 4 servings.

——PORK IN CIDER & ORANGE——

3 tablespoons olive oil
Flour for coating
Salt and pepper
1 (1-1/2-lb.) boned and rolled pork loin roast
1 small Spanish onion, sliced
1-1/2 cups hard cider
Juice of 1 large orange
Zest of 1/4 orange, cut into fine strips
Pinch of ground cinnamon
Pinch of sugar, if desired
Thin orange slices, herb sprigs and toasted slivered
    almonds, to garnish

In a heavy large pan, heat oil. Put flour on a plate and season with salt and pepper. Roll pork in seasoned flour to coat evenly and lightly. Add to pan and brown evenly, about 10 minutes. Remove and keep warm. Stir onion into pan and cook over low heat about 20 minutes, stirring occasionally, until very soft and lightly browned. Stir in cider, orange juice and zest strips and cinnamon. Bring to a boil, reduce heat and simmer 2 to 3 minutes.

Return pork to pan, turn it in sauce, cover and simmer about 45 minutes or until pork is tender and juices run clear when tested with the tip of a knife. Transfer pork to a serving dish and boil sauce, if necessary, to thicken lightly. Taste for seasoning and add a pinch sugar, if necessary. Pour sauce over pork and garnish with orange slices and slivered almonds.

Makes 4 servings.

SPICED PORK LOIN

1 tablespoon paprika
3 garlic cloves, finely crushed
1 teaspoon chopped fresh oregano
1/2 teaspoon finely crushed cumin seeds
1 bay leaf, crushed
Salt
3 tablespoons extra-virgin olive oil
1 (1-1/2-lb.) boned and rolled pork loin roast
2 tablespoons olive oil
1/4 cup full-bodied dry white wine
Pitted green olives, to serve

In a small bowl, mix together paprika, garlic, oregano, cumin seeds, bay leaf and salt. Stir in olive oil.

Rub spice mixture well into pork. Place in a non-metallic dish, cover and refrigerate 2 to 5 days. Bring pork to room temperature 30 minutes before cooking.

Cut pork into 4 slices. In a skillet over medium-high heat, heat oil. Add pork and brown quickly on both sides, then reduce heat and cook 4 to 5 minutes on each side until cooked through. Transfer slices to a warm serving plate. Stir wine into cooking juices, boil 2 to 3 minutes, then pour over pork. Scatter green olives over the top.

Makes 4 servings.

—— VEAL WITH ANCHOVIES ——

1/2 cup olive oil
Flour for coating
Salt and pepper
4 veal loin chops, 3/4 inch thick
2 small garlic cloves, coarsely chopped
2 canned anchovy fillets, drained and chopped
2 tablespoons chopped fresh parsley
1-1/2 tablespoons coarsely chopped capers
Squeeze of lemon juice
Parsley and lemon slices, to garnish

In a skillet large enough to hold chops in a single layer, heat 1/4 cup of the oil. Season chops with salt and pepper, then coat with flour.

Add chops to pan and cook about 10 minutes, turning occasionally, until light brown and crisp on outsides and just cooked in centers.

Meanwhile, in a small saucepan, heat remaining oil. Add garlic and cook until garlic is pale gold. Stir in anchovies and parsley. Cook 20 to 30 seconds, mashing and stirring anchovies with a wooden spoon. Add capers, and pepper and lemon juice to taste. Transfer chops to a warmed plate and top with sauce. Serve garnished with parsley and lemon slices.

Makes 4 servings.

RICE & CHICKEN

3 tablespoons olive oil
1 (3-lb.) chicken, cut into 8 pieces, or 4 large chicken
  pieces, halved
1 Spanish onion, finely chopped
2 garlic cloves, chopped
1 large red bell pepper, cut into strips
1 tablespoon paprika
1-1/2 cups peeled, seeded and chopped beefsteak
  tomatoes
2 cups short-grain white rice
1/4 teaspoon saffron threads, finely crushed
3-3/4 cups boiling chicken stock or water
1 cup small shelled fresh or frozen green peas
2 tablespoons chopped fresh parsley
Lime wedges, to serve

In a paella pan or large skillet, heat oil. Add chicken and cook about 10 minutes or until a light golden color all over. Remove and set aside. Add onion, garlic and bell pepper to pan and simmer 8 to 10 minutes until vegetables are soft. Stir in paprika and heat 30 to 60 seconds, then add tomatoes and cook about 10 minutes or until mixture is thick.

Add rice and stir 2 minutes. Add saffron and stock or water and quickly bring to a boil. Return chicken to pan, reduce heat and simmer 15 minutes. Add peas if using fresh ones and simmer about 10 minutes or until chicken and rice are tender and most of liquid has been absorbed. Add frozen peas, if using. Remove from heat, cover pan and leave 5 to 10 minutes. Sprinkle with parsley. Serve straight from pan if a paella pan has been used. Serve with lime wedges.

Makes 4 servings.

PAELLA

1/4 cup olive oil
2 pounds chicken, cut into small pieces
2 Spanish onions, chopped
4 garlic cloves, chopped
1 tablespoon paprika
2 cups short-grain white rice
3 beefsteak tomatoes, peeled, seeded and chopped
7-1/2 cups boiling chicken stock
Large pinch of saffron threads, finely crushed
1 rosemary sprig
Salt and pepper
8 ounces small squid
5 ounces green beans
1 pound mussels in their shells
8 ounces raw shrimp in their shells
4 ounces fresh fava beans

In a 16-inch paella or 4-quart wide shallow pan, heat oil. Add chicken and cook about 10 minutes or until lightly browned. Add onion and garlic and fry 5 minutes, then stir in paprika followed by rice. Stir 2 to 3 minutes. Stir in tomatoes, stock, rosemary, salt and pepper. Dissolve saffron in 2 tablespoons stock, then add to paella. Boil 8 to 10 minutes.

Prepare squid (see page 17). Cut bodies into rings and chop tentacles. Cut green beans into short pieces. Arrange all seafood, green beans and fava beans over paella; do not stir. Gradually reduce heat and simmer 8 to 10 minutes or until rice is tender and liquid absorbed. Cover, remove from heat and leave 5 to 10 minutes before serving.

Makes 4 servings.

FIDEUA

3 to 4 tablespoons olive oil
1-1/4 pounds large raw shrimp
9 ounces monkfish fillet, cut into pieces
Salt
1-1/2 teaspoons paprika
1-1/2 cups peeled, seeded and chopped beefsteak
    tomatoes
5-1/2 cups fish stock
2 garlic cloves
1 tablespoon chopped fresh parsley
6 to 8 saffron threads, finely crushed
9 ounces spaghettini, broken into pieces
Lemon wedges and sprigs of fresh parsley, to garnish

In a large paella pan or large skillet, heat 3 tablespoons oil. Add shrimp and cook, stirring, 2 to 3 minutes, then remove and set aside.

Add monkfish to pan and cook a few minutes or until lightly browned all over. Season with salt. Remove and set aside.

Add more oil to pan, if necessary. Stir in paprika and cook 30 to 60 seconds, then add tomatoes. Cook about 5 minutes, stirring occasionally. Add stock and bring to a boil.

Using a mortar and pestle, pound garlic, parsley and saffron together. Stir in a little hot stock, then stir into pan and boil 2 minutes. Add spaghettini and boil until pasta has absorbed most of the stock and is just tender.

Arrange monkfish and shrimp in the spaghettini and cook until hot, then remove from heat. Cover pan and let stand 5 minutes before serving. Garnish with lemon wedges and parsley and serve from pan if a paella pan has been used.

Makes 4 servings.

——— RICE & BLACK BEANS ———

2 tablespoons olive oil
1 Spanish onion, chopped
2 garlic cloves, chopped
4 ounces unsmoked slab bacon, chopped
1 small red bell pepper, chopped
1 teaspoon paprika
2 cups peeled, seeded and chopped beefsteak tomatoes
Salt and pepper
1-1/3 cups short-grain white rice
Fresh herb sprigs, to garnish
BLACK BEANS:
1-1/3 cups dried black beans, soaked overnight and
    drained
1/2 Spanish onion
2 garlic cloves, crushed

To prepare the beans, put them in a saucepan with onion and garlic. Cover with water, bring to a boil and boil 10 minutes. Reduce heat, cover and simmer 1-1/2 to 2 hours or until just tender. Meanwhile in a saucepan, heat oil. Add onion, garlic, bacon and bell pepper, and cook, stirring occasionally, until bacon begins to brown. Stir in paprika 30 to 60 seconds, then stir in tomatoes and cook about 5 minutes, stirring occasionally. Season with salt and pepper.

Drain beans. Discard onion and garlic. Stir rice and 2 cups water into pan with tomato mixture. Bring to a boil, stir, cover and simmer about 25 minutes or until liquid is absorbed and rice is tender. Stir in the beans. Taste for seasoning and serve garnished with herb sprigs.

Makes 4 to 6 servings.

SPICED RICE & PEPPERS

1/4 cup olive oil
1-1/3 cups long-grain white rice
2 garlic cloves
Salt
1 teaspoon each cumin seeds and coriander seeds
3 tablespoons tomato paste
2 teaspoons paprika
1 teaspoon chili powder
Pinch of saffron threads, crushed and dissolved in 2
　　tablespoons boiling water
2-1/2 cups boiling chicken stock, vegetable stock or
　　water
3 or 4 red bell peppers, roasted, peeled and halved
　　(page 10)
Extra-virgin olive oil to serve, if desired
Fresh herbs, to garnish

In a paella pan or a wide, shallow saucepan,
heat oil. Stir in rice and stir-fry 2 to 3
minutes. Meanwhile, using a mortar and
pestle, grind together garlic, salt, cumin
seeds and coriander seeds. Stir in tomato
paste, paprika, chili powder and saffron
liquid. Stir into rice. Stir in stock or water.
Bring to a boil, then reduce heat, cover and
simmer about 7 minutes.

Arrange peppers around sides of pan. Simmer
7 to 10 minutes until rice is tender and plump
and liquid is absorbed. Remove from heat and
let stand 5 minutes. Drizzle extra-virgin oil
over pepper, if desired, and garnish with
herbs.

Makes 4 servings.

RICE WITH CHICKPEAS

12 ounces chickpeas, soaked overnight and drained
Olive oil for frying
3 garlic cloves, finely chopped
1-1/3 cups short-grain white rice
2-1/2 cups chicken stock or water
1 recipe Tomato Sauce (page 115)
Chopped fresh herbs, to garnish

Simmer chickpeas in plenty of water 1-1/2 to 2 hours or until just tender.

Meanwhile, prepare the rice. In a saucepan, heat 2 tablespoons oil. Add garlic and fry 2 minutes. Stir in rice and stir-fry 3 to 4 minutes, then stir in 1-1/4 cups stock or water. Simmer 10 minutes, then add another 1-1/4 cups stock or water. Continue cooking 10 to 12 minutes or until liquid is absorbed and rice is tender. Cover and keep warm.

Drain chickpeas. In a skillet, heat about 1/2-inch layer of oil. Add chickpeas and fry, stirring frequently, until golden-brown. Stir into rice, then transfer to a warmed serving dish. Pour Tomato Sauce over chickpeas and rice. Garnish with herbs and serve.

Makes 4 servings.

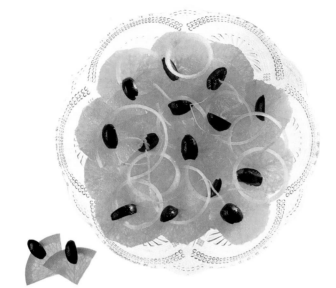

—VALENCIAN ORANGE SALAD—

4 large oranges
1/2 Spanish onion, thinly sliced
2 tablespoons white-wine vinegar
1/3 cup extra-virgin olive oil
Salt and pepper
Pinch of sugar
Pitted ripe olives, to garnish

With a sharp knife, peel oranges and cut away pith and membrane from outsides. Thinly slice oranges and remove seeds.

Separate onion slices into rings. Arrange orange and onion slices on a plate.

In a small bowl, mix together vinegar, oil, salt, pepper and sugar. Pour dressing over the orange and onion slices. Sprinkle olives over the top, cover and refrigerate 30 minutes before serving.

Makes 4 to 6 servings.

ASPARAGUS WITH EGG

1-1/2 pounds fresh asparagus
1 hard-cooked egg, finely chopped
1/3 cup olive oil
1 garlic clove
3/4 cup fresh, coarse bread crumbs
2 tablespoons chopped fresh parsley

Using a small sharp knife, cut off woody part at end of asparagus stems. Working from tip to bottom, scrape off scales from stems. Tie stems into 4 bundles with kitchen string.

In a deep saucepan, bring 2 inches of water to a boil. Add asparagus bundles, tips pointing upward. Cover pan with a lid or dome of foil and simmer 8 to 10 minutes or until asparagus is just tender. Remove asparagus and untie bundles. Drain asparagus on a thick pad of paper towels. Arrange on a warm serving plate, sprinkle egg over stems, cover and keep warm.

Meanwhile, in a skillet, heat oil. Add garlic and fry until lightly browned. Discard garlic. Stir bread crumbs into pan and cook 5 to 7 minutes, stirring, until crisp and golden. Remove from heat and stir in parsley, then pour it over the asparagus, leaving tips uncovered. Serve immediately.

Makes 4 servings.

——SPINACH WITH RAISINS——

1/3 cup raisins
2 pounds fresh spinach
3 tablespoons olive oil
1 garlic clove, finely chopped
3 tablespoons pine nuts
Salt and pepper
Croutons, to serve

Into a small bowl, put raisins. Cover with boiling water and let soak.

Rinse spinach well, then shake off surplus water but do not dry the leaves. Into a large saucepan, put spinach. Cover and cook until spinach wilts. Uncover and cook until excess moisture has evaporated. Chop coarsely. Drain raisins.

In a skillet, heat oil. Add garlic and pine nuts and fry, stirring occasionally, until beginning to color. Stir in spinach and raisins, season with salt and pepper and cook over low heat 5 minutes. Serve with croutons sprinkled over the top.

Makes 4 servings.

PISTO MANCHEGO

2 tablespoons olive oil
2 bacon slices, chopped
2 large onions, chopped
1 garlic clove, chopped
2 zucchini, chopped
4 red bell peppers, chopped
3 cups peeled, seeded and chopped beefsteak tomatoes
Bunch of mint, parsley and basil, chopped
Salt and black pepper
4 poached or fried eggs, to serve (optional)

In a large skillet, heat oil. Add bacon, onions and garlic and cook about 15 minutes, stirring occasionally, until onions are very soft and lightly colored.

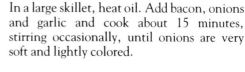

Add zucchini and bell pepper to pan and fry about 4 minutes or until soft. Stir in tomatoes and herbs and cook 20 to 30 minutes or until thickened. Season to taste with salt and black pepper. Serve topped by poached or fried eggs, if desired.

Makes 4 servings.

——FAVA BEANS WITH HAM——

2 tablespoons olive oil
4 large green onions, finely chopped
1 red bell pepper, seeded and diced
2 ounces serrano ham, diced
2-1/2 cups shelled fava beans
About 3/4 cup dry white wine
Salt and black pepper
Chopped fresh herbs, to garnish

In a saucepan, heat oil. Add green onions, bell pepper and ham and cook 3 minutes.

Stir in beans and cook 1 minute. Add enough wine to cover; bring to a boil, then cover pan and simmer about 20 minutes or until beans are tender.

Uncover and boil off excess liquid. Add season with salt, if needed, and black pepper. Cool slightly before serving. Garnish with chopped herbs.

Makes 4 servings.

—BAKED MIXED VEGETABLES—

2-1/4 cups thinly sliced eggplants (1 pound)
Salt and black pepper
2/3 cup olive oil
3 garlic cloves, crushed
3 cups peeled, seeded and chopped beefsteak tomatoes
1 tablespoon tomato paste
2 Spanish onions, thinly sliced
1 green bell pepper, sliced
1 pound potatoes, boiled and sliced
1/2 cup fresh bread crumbs

In a colander, sprinkle eggplant slices with salt and leave 30 minutes. Rinse under cold running water and dry well on paper towels. Meanwhile, in a saucepan, heat 1 tablespoon of the oil. Add garlic and fry gently without browning. Add tomatoes, tomato paste, salt and black pepper. Cover and simmer 15 minutes. Meanwhile, preheat oven to 400F (205C). In a skillet, heat 4 tablespoons of the oil.

Add onions and bell pepper and cook 15 minutes, stirring occasionally. Using a slotted spoon, remove from pan; set aside. Add remaining oil to pan. Add eggplant slices in batches and fry until golden. Drain on paper towels. Layer all the vegetables in a baking dish, season each layer with salt and black pepper and moisten with the tomato sauce. Finish with tomato sauce. Sprinkle with bread crumbs. Bake about 20 minutes or until golden.

Makes 4 to 6 servings.

HERBED PEAS

2 tablespoons olive oil
1 onion, finely chopped
2 garlic cloves, chopped
1-1/2 cups shelled fresh green peas
1/2 cup dry white wine
Bouquet garni of 2 fresh parsley sprigs, 1 fresh thyme
　　sprig and 1 bay leaf
8 saffron threads
Salt and black pepper
Strips of red bell pepper and mint sprigs, to garnish

In a large pan, heat oil. Add onion and cook about 5 minutes, stirring occasionally, until soft but not colored. Add 1 garlic clove and cook 1 minute, then stir in peas, wine and bouquet garni. Heat until simmering, then cover and simmer about 15 minutes or until peas are tender. Discard bouquet garni.

Using a mortar and pestle, crush together remaining garlic, the saffron and a pinch of salt to make a smooth paste. Stir in a little of the cooking liquid, then stir mixture into peas. Add black pepper and cook a few more minutes. Serve garnished with strips of bell pepper and mint sprigs.

Makes 4 servings.

— POTATOES WITH CHORIZO —

1/4 cup olive oil
4 ounces chorizo, chopped
4 cups coarsely chopped potatoes (1-1/2 pounds)
1 Spanish onion, chopped
1 red bell pepper, seeded and chopped
2-1/2 cups peeled, seeded and chopped beefsteak
    tomatoes
Salt and black pepper
Chicken stock, veal stock or water, to cover
Mint sprigs, to garnish

In a large pan, heat oil. Add chorizo and cook, stirring occasionally, until lightly browned. Remove chorizo with a slotted spoon.

Add potatoes and onion and cook, stirring occasionally, 5 minutes. Stir in bell pepper and cook 5 minutes, then add tomatoes and return chorizo to pan. Season with salt and black pepper.

Just cover with stock or water and simmer about 15 minutes or until potatoes are tender and most of the liquid has been absorbed. Garnish with mint sprigs and serve.

Makes 4 servings.

BROCCOLI WITH CHILES

1 pound broccoli
Olive oil
2 garlic cloves, sliced
2 dried red chiles, seeded and crushed
Salt

With a sharp knife, cut thick broccoli stems in half or thirds lengthwise. Add all of broccoli to a saucepan of boiling salted water and boil 2 minutes, then drain and rinse under cold running water.

In a heavy skillet large enough to hold broccoli in a single layer, heat oil. Add garlic and chiles to pan. Cook over medium heat 3 to 4 minutes or until sizzling.

Add broccoli and turn to coat in oil and then reduce heat to very low. Pour in 1/2 cup water, add salt and cover tightly. Simmer about 20 minutes, turning broccoli carefully 2 or 3 times or until broccoli is tender. If necessary, uncover and boil off excess liquid. Serve hot or warm.

Makes 4 servings.

CHURROS

Olive oil or other vegetable oil for deep-frying
Mixture of vanilla sugar and powdered sugar for
  dusting
Lemon zest and mint sprigs, to decorate
Spanish Hot Chocolate (page 117), to serve
DOUGH:
1 cup minus 2 tablespoons self-rising flour
1/4 teaspoon ground cinnamon
1/4 cup butter, diced
3/4 cup water
3 eggs, beaten

To make dough, onto a plate, sift flour and cinnamon together. Place beside the stove.

In a saucepan, gently heat butter and water until butter has melted, then bring quickly to a boil. Immediately remove from heat and quickly add flour mixture all at once and beat vigorously until smooth. Return to heat about 30 seconds, still beating. Remove from heat and cool slightly. Gradually beat in eggs until mixture is a smooth, thick glossy paste. Half fill a deep-fryer or pan with oil and heat to 375F (190C).

Spoon dough into a pastry bag fitted with a 1/4- to 1/2-inch plain tip and pipe 3 or 4 pieces into the hot oil, forming them into rings, spirals or U-shapes; use a sharp knife to cut off mixture at required length. Fry about 3 minutes, turning once, or until golden. Using a slotted spoon, transfer to paper towels to drain. Keep warm while frying remaining mixture. Dust with sugar mixture and decorate with lemon zest and mint. Serve hot with Spanish Hot Chocolate.

Makes 4 servings.

APPLE CAKE

2 cups plus 2 tablespoons self-rising flour
3/4 teaspoon ground cinnamon
1/3 cup sugar
Finely grated zest and juice 1 lemon
2 eggs, beaten
3 tablespoons sweet sherry
2/3 cup olive oil
1 pound Granny Smith apples

Preheat oven to 350F (175C). Grease a 7-inch pan. In a bowl, stir together flour, cinnamon, sugar and lemon zest. Make a well in the center and gradually add eggs, sherry, olive oil and lemon juice, stirring to make a smooth batter.

With a sharp knife, peel, core and chop apples. Fold into cake batter, then spoon batter into prepared pan. Bake 40 to 45 minutes or until golden-brown and firm to the touch in center. Cool in pan a few minutes, then turn out onto a wire rack to cool completely.

Makes 8 servings.

FRIED CUSTARD

About 3 tablespoons sugar
3 eggs
1/2 cup all-purpose flour
1 cup whipping cream
1 cup milk
Few drops of vanilla extract
1-1/2 cups cake crumbs, preferably lemon cake
Vegetable oil for deep-frying
Orange slices and zest, to decorate

Lightly flour an 11″ x 7″ baking pan. In a bowl, beat together sugar and 2 eggs until pale. Gradually stir in flour.

In a heavy, preferably nonstick, saucepan, heat cream, milk and vanilla extract to a boil. Slowly pour into the egg mixture, stirring. Return to heat and simmer, stirring, until thickened; do not boil. Pour onto baking pan to make an even layer about 1/2 inch thick, then cool. Cover and refrigerate at least 1 hour. Cut cold custard mixture into 1-inch squares, rectangles or diamonds.

Beat remaining egg. Dip shapes first in beaten egg, then in the crumbs. Half fill a deep-fryer or pan with vegetable oil and heat to 375F (190C). Add coated shapes in batches and cook about 1-1/2 minutes or until golden and crisp on outside; keep oil temperature up because the cubes should cook very quickly. Using a slotted spoon, transfer to paper towels, drain quickly and serve immediately. Decorate with orange slices and zest.

Makes 4 to 6 servings.

ORANGE FLANS

Grated zest of 1 orange
1-1/4 cups fresh orange juice
3 whole eggs
3 egg yolks
2 tablespoons sugar
Orange slices and fresh mint, to decorate
CARAMEL:
1/2 cup superfine sugar
1 tablespoon water

In a small bowl, put orange zest and orange juice. Set aside to soak. Meanwhile, preheat oven to 350F (175C). Warm 4 ramekin dishes.

To make the caramel, in a small, heavy saucepan, gently heat sugar and water, swirling pan until sugar has dissolved. Cook until golden-brown. Immediately pour one-quarter into each ramekin and swirl them around so caramel coats sides and bottoms. Put in a baking pan. Gently heat orange juice and orange zest until just below a simmer.

Meanwhile, in a bowl, whisk whole eggs and egg yolks with sugar until thick, Slowly pour in orange juice and zest, whisking constantly. Divide among ramekins, then pour boiling water around them. Cover dishes with waxed paper and bake about 25 minutes or until lightly set. Remove dishes from pan and refrigerate until cold. Just before serving, unmold desserts onto cold plates. Decorate with orange slices and mint.

Makes 4 servings.

SPANISH RICE PUDDING

About 6-1/4 cups milk
1 cinnamon stick
2 or 3 strips lemon zest
Pinch of salt
1/2 cup short-grain white rice
1/3 cup sugar

Set aside 1/2 cup milk. In a large saucepan, heat remaining milk, cinnamon stick, lemon zest and salt to a boil. Stir in rice.

Reduce heat so milk just simmers and cook 15 minutes, stirring constantly, then cook, uncovered, about 1 hour, stirring occasionally. Stir in sugar.

Cook 1 hour, stirring occasionally, or until milk has been absorbed and pudding is very creamy and falls easily from a spoon. Add some of reserved milk if mixture is too thick. Discard cinnamon stick and lemon zest. Serve warm, at room temperature or lightly chilled.

Makes 6 servings.

Variation: Serve with fresh fruit and a sprinkling of cinnamon, if desired.

BUNUELOS

5 tablespoons each milk and water
2 tablespoons each butter and sugar
1/3 cup self-rising flour
Grated zest of 1 lemon
2 eggs, beaten
1 tablespoon brandy
Olive oil for deep-frying
2 tablespoons powdered sugar
1 teaspoon ground cinnamon
FILLING:
1/3 cup sugar
3/4 cup all-purpose flour
2 eggs, beaten
2-1/4 cups milk
Grated zest of 1 lemon
3 tablespoons butter

To make filling, in a bowl, stir together sugar, flour, eggs and a little milk. In a heavy, preferably nonstick, saucepan, heat lemon zest and remaining milk to a boil. Slowly pour into flour mixture, stirring. Return to pan. Cook over low heat, stirring with a wooden spoon, until sauce thickens, then continue to cook 5 minutes, stirring. Do not boil. Remove from heat, stir in butter, cover closely with waxed paper and refrigerate.

Prepare dough according to directions on page 108, melting butter in milk and water and adding brandy with eggs. Heat oil in a deep-fryer to 350F (175C). Form dough into small walnut-size balls and fry in batches until evenly browned. Transfer to paper towels while frying remaining mixture. Pierce a hole in the side of each ball and pipe filling into holes. Serve hot, thickly dusted with sugar mixture.

Makes 4 servings.

ROMESCO SAUCE

3 garlic cloves, unpeeled
8 ounces beefsteak tomatoes
1 fresh red bell pepper
1/3 cup blanched almonds, lightly toasted
1 dried hot red chile, soaked in cold water 30 minutes,
   drained and seeded
3 tablespoons red-wine vinegar
About 2/3 cup olive oil
Salt

Preheat oven to its hottest setting. Roast garlic, tomatoes and bell pepper 20 to 30 minutes, removing tomatoes and garlic when soft and pepper when soft and lightly browned.

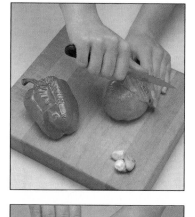

With a sharp knife, peel tomatoes and pepper and discard seeds. Peel garlic. In a blender or food processor with the metal blade, process vegetables with almonds and chile. With the motor running, slowly pour in vinegar and enough oil to make a thick sauce.

Add salt to taste. Cover and refrigerate 3 to 4 hours before serving with meat, fish and vegetable dishes.

Makes 6 servings.

Variation: True Romesco Sauce is made from romesco peppers. If available, substitute 2 dried romesco peppers for the red bell pepper and chile.

TOMATO SAUCE

2 tablespoons olive oil
1/2 Spanish onion, finely chopped
1/2 garlic clove, chopped
1 red bell pepper, seeded and chopped
6 cups peeled, seeded and chopped beefsteak tomatoes
Sugar or tomato paste (optional)
Salt and black pepper

In a skillet, heat oil. Add onion and cook over low heat 5 minutes.

Stir in garlic and bell pepper and cook 10 minutes, stirring occasionally.

Stir tomatoes into pan. Simmer 20 to 30 minutes, stirring occasionally, until thickened. Add sugar or tomato paste, if desired, and season with salt and black pepper. Process in a blender or food processor with the metal blade until pureed, or press through a non-metallic strainer, if desired.

Makes 4 to 6 servings.

─SPANISH COUNTRY BREAD─

2 cups bread flour
2 teaspoons salt
1 envelope active dried yeast (about 1 tablespoon)
3/4 cup warm water
Olive oil for brushing
Cornmeal for sprinkling

Into a large bowl, sift flour and salt. Stir in yeast and form a well in center. Slowly pour water into well, stirring with a wooden spoon, to make a dough. Beat well until dough comes away from sides of bowl.

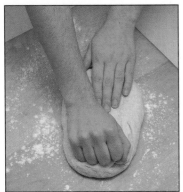

Turn dough out onto a lightly floured surface and knead 10 to 15 minutes or until smooth and elastic; add a little more flour if dough is sticky. Put dough in an oiled bowl, cover and leave in a warm place, about 2-1/2 hours or until doubled in volume. Lightly sprinkle a baking sheet with cornmeal. Turn dough onto lightly floured surface and punch down, then roll to a 16″ x 6″ rectangle. Roll up like a jellyroll and pinch seam to seal.

Place roll, seam-side down, on baking sheet. Using a very sharp knife, make 3 diagonal slashes on roll at equal distances. Brush top lightly with water. Leave in a warm place about 1 hour or until doubled in volume. Preheat oven to 450F (225C). Place a pan of water in the bottom of oven. Brush loaf again with water and bake 5 minutes. Remove pan of water. Brush loaf once more with water. Bake about 20 minutes or until loaf sounds hollow when tapped on bottom.

Makes 1 loaf.

—SPANISH HOT CHOCOLATE—

3 ounces semisweet chocolate, broken into pieces
2 cups milk
Cinnamon sticks and orange zest, to decorate

Into the top of a double boiler or a bowl placed over a saucepan of hot water, place chocolate and heat until melted.

In a saucepan, heat milk to a boil. Using a wooden spoon, slowly stir a little boiling milk into chocolate.

Using a wire whisk, whisk in remaining milk and continue to whisk until mixture is frothy. Pour into heatproof glasses or cups and decorate with cinnamon sticks and orange zest.

Makes 2 servings.

Variation: Rub cubed sugar over a whole orange to remove the zest, then add the sugar to the hot chocolate.

HORCHATA

8 ounces tiger nuts
4-1/2 cups water
Finely grated zest of 1/2 lemon
About 1/3 cup sugar
Lemon slices, to decorate

Rinse nuts well under cold running water. Soak in clean water overnight. Drain.

In a blender or food processor with the metal blade, process nuts with enough of the water to make a fine paste. Add remaining water, lemon zest and sugar to taste.

Refrigerate 4 hours. Strain the liquid through a cheesecloth-lined strainer. Refrigerate until very cold. Pour into glasses; decorate with lemon slices.

Makes 4 servings.

Note: Tiger nuts, also called chufas, are small dried tubers. They can be found in Spanish and some Latin American markets. If unavailable, use almonds or cashew nuts.

SANGRIA

1 (750-ml) bottle red wine, chilled
2 strips orange zest
2 strips lemon zest
2 tablespoons sugar
Juice of 4 oranges
Juice of 2 lemons
3 cups soda water, chilled
Fresh mint sprigs and orange and lemon slices, to
    decorate

Into a large cold bowl, put 6 to 8 ice cubes, pour in the wine and add orange and lemon zest.

Into a small bowl, put orange juice. Add sugar and stir until sugar dissolves. Stir into wine with lemon juice. Pour into a large, cold serving pitcher. Add soda water. Decorate with mint sprigs and orange and lemon slices.

Makes 4 servings.

INDEX

Apple Cake, 109
Artichoke & Ham Tortilla, 46
Asparagus with Egg, 100

Baked Mixed Vegetables, 104
Baked Sea Bream, 64
Beef in Spinach Sauce, 85
Beef with Tomato Sauce, 86
Bell Pepper & Onion Tart, 22
Braised Lamb & Vegetables, 84
Broccoli with Chiles, 107
Broiled Shrimp, 14
Bunuelos, 113

Cheese Fritters, 21
Chicken in Sanfaina Sauce, 66
Chicken in Vinegar Sauce, 70
Chicken Pepitoria, 71
Chicken with Garlic Sauce, 72
Chicken with Parsley, 65
Chicken with Sherry, 67
Chicken with Walnut Sauce, 69
Churros, 108
Cod & Eggplant Stew, 60
Cod with Parsley Crust, 58

Duck & Olives, 78
Duck with Pears, 76

Eggs Flamenca, 45
Empanada, 24

Fava Beans with Ham, 103
Fideua, 94
Fish in Green Sauce, 59
Fried Cauliflower, 32
Fried Custard, 110
Fried Stuffed Peppers, 33

Garlic Beef, 87
Gazpacho, 41
Green Mussel Salad, 18

Hake with Peas & Potatoes, 57
Halibut in White Sauce, 56
Herbed Peas, 105
Horchata, 118

Kidneys in Sherry, 26

Lamb Chilindron, 79
Lamb in Herb Sauce, 82
Lamb with Lemon & Garlic, 83
Lamb with Ripe Olives, 80
Leek Salad, 38
Lentil & Chorizo Soup, 42

Marinated Sardines, 20
Monkfish & Almond Sauce, 49
Monkfish & Artichokes, 50
Monkfish with Paprika, 48
Mullet with Anchovy Sauce, 55
Mushrooms with Anchovies, 30
Mushrooms with Garlic, 29

Orange Flans, 111

Paella, 93
Pisto Manchego, 102
Pork in Cider & Orange, 89
Pork with Herb Sauce, 88
Potatoes with Chorizo, 106
Potatoes with Garlic Sauce, 34
Potatoes with Red Sauce, 35

Quail with Grapes, 73

Rice & Black Beans, 96
Rice & Chicken, 92
Rice with Chickpeas, 98
Roast Monkfish & Garlic, 52
Roasted Pepper Salad, 37
Roasted Vegetable Salad, 36
Romesco Sauce, 114

Sangria, 119
Scrambled Eggs & Shrimp, 44
Shrimp in Overcoats, 15
Shrimp-Stuffed Eggs, 31
Sizzling Shrimp, 13
Skate with Red Pepper, 61
Sole with Green Dressing, 53
Spanish Country Bread, 116
Spanish Hot Chocolate, 117
Spanish Partridges, 74
Spanish Rice Pudding, 112
Spice-Coated Lamb, 81
Spiced Olives, 28
Spiced Pork Loin, 90
Spiced Rice & Peppers, 97
Spicy Chicken, 68
Spicy Chickpea Soup, 43
Spicy Pork Kabobs, 27
Spinach with Raisins, 101
Stuffed Mussels, 12
Stuffed Squid, 17

Tomato Sauce, 115
Tortilla with Red Pepper, 47
Trout with Ham, 54
Tuna Croquettes, 16
Tuna Salad, 19

Valencian Orange Salad, 99
Veal with Anchovies, 91
Vegetable Salad, 39

White Soup with Grapes, 40

Zarzuela, 62